Praise for
RECONCILIATION RECONSIDERED

"This book has something to say and it deserves to be heard by all followers of Jesus. The author has gathered together outstanding scholars who speak with truth and candor—all couched in love—and give us further perspective on the issue of race relations in the Christian community."

—**Royce Money**, Chancellor Abilene Christian University

"A powerful collection of essays about the very heart of the American character: religion and race. This important volume does exactly as it proposes to do—advance the national conversation on race. Beautifully edited, this volume is a must read for anyone interested in better understanding race and faith in the United States."

—**Michael O. Emerson**, co-author of *Divided by Faith* and *United by Faith*

Reconciliation Reconsidered

Advancing the National Conversation on Race in Churches of Christ

Edited by
TANYA SMITH BRICE

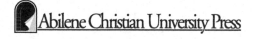

Abilene Christian University Press

RECONCILIATION RECONSIDERED

Advancing the National Conversation on Race in Churches of Christ

ACU PRESS

Cover design by Cynithea Reeder
Interior text design by Sandy Armstrong, Strong Design

For information contact:
Abilene Christian University Press
ACU Box 29138
Abilene, Texas 79699

1-877-816-4455 toll free
www.acupressbooks.com

16 17 18 19 20 21 22 / 7 6 5 4 3 2 1

In Loving Memory of

Albert Lemon Smith

Wilma Sullivan Smith

Wilbert Smith

Nathan Mark Fleer

Acknowledgements

This volume of essays is the result of years of working towards a tangible response to the segregated congregations of the Churches of Christ. I am the granddaughter of Albert Lemon Smith and Wilma Sullivan Smith. My grandfather was a Church of Christ minister who planted several African American congregations in South Carolina and Georgia. Although I grew up in the Churches of Christ, I never really thought about white congregations of Churches of Christ. I remember going with my grandfather to a white congregation to teach them to sing certain songs. As I grew older, I attended African American congregations that had quarterly or semi-annual joint "sing a longs" with a local white congregation in an effort to demonstrate unity. I participated in women's ministry programs sponsored by African American congregations that required the visible participation of white women from white congregations to demonstrate unity.

In 2006, I joined the faculty of Abilene Christian University (ACU). It was here that I was introduced to United By Faith (UBF), a reading group of ACU administrators, faculty, and staff. This multiracial group, primarily led by Doug Foster, met monthly in each other's homes to discuss racial reconciliation in the Churches of Christ over a potluck meal. I honestly never thought about, nor did I find problematic, our racially segregated congregations prior to my involvement with this group. It was a combination of my participation in UBF, as well as my family's intentional decision to worship with a white congregation, that I realized that black and white congregations are doctrinally and traditionally different. I am thankful to Doug Foster and to the UBF participants (whom I will not attempt to name for fear that I will forget someone) for helping me to better understand the foundation of my faith, and for demonstrating grace and patience as I worked through my theological questions.

During the summer of 2010, I was invited to participate in the Power of Race in American Religion Seminar at Calvin College, in Grand Rapids, Michigan. This seminar was facilitated by Michael Emerson, co-author of the book entitled, *United By Faith*, after which the group in Abilene was named. Emerson brought together scholars from different denominations, parts of the country, and academic disciplines to engage in research on race in religion. It is in this seminar that I began examining the racialized history of Churches of Christ. I am thankful to Michael Emerson and all of the seminar participants (Ryon Cobb, Kimberly Hill, Karen Johnson, Phillip Sinitiere, Rusty Hawkins, Julie Park, Jerry Park, Bruce Fields, Erica Wong, Mark Mulder, Paul Gordiejew, Rebecca Kim, Regina Shands-Stoltzfus, and Luke Harlow) for allowing me to talk incessantly about my discoveries of Church of Christ history as found in primary documents.

My dear brother in the faith, Jerry Taylor, of Abilene, Texas, introduced me to the formalized work of advancing the national conversation on race among Churches of Christ through his National Freedom in Christ conferences. Taylor insisted that I participate in these sessions, primarily made up of ministers and church leaders (read: male), which challenged my sense of my role as a woman in the Churches of Christ. Taylor continues to push me as we journey on this road together.

I am thankful for the National Strategic Planning Team, facilitated by Joey Cope. This team is made up of ministers and church leaders from around the country to engage in intentional efforts towards racial reconciliation. We developed vision and mission statements as well as a strategic plan. Three strategies for carrying out this work has been developed: Spiritual Growth and Spiritual Centeredness; Research, Education & Communication; and, Intentionality and Action. This book is one output of that strategic plan. The Racial Unity Leadership Summits are another output. And, the Civil Rights section of the Christian Scholars Conference is yet another output of the national strategic plan.

I am so thankful for David Fleer, and his role as Director of the Christian Scholars Conference. He convinced me to lead the Civil Rights section, which provides scholarly examinations of racial reconciliation in the churches of the Stone-Campbell movement. This section has produced several of the essays in this book. It was Fleer who moved this book project from conversations to a published product. I am thankful to Jason Fikes, Director of the ACU Press, who took on the challenge to publish this book. I am grateful for his willingness to work with me throughout this process.

I must acknowledge my family who has been supportive of all of my scholarly endeavors. I am thankful to my husband, Boston Brice III, to my daughter, Tyler Alexis, and to my son, Boston IV, for putting up with me over the past several years, either heading to an airport to present on topics related to racial reconciliation, or sitting on my laptop writing about racial reconciliation. It is my prayer that this book will serve as a useful tool for my children as they evolve into our future church. I am thankful to each of my siblings: Lorraine Smith Davis, Michael Smith, Stoney Smith, Samuel Smith, Jr., and Samantha Smith, for their support. I am thankful to my parents, Samuel Smith, Sr. and Mabel Conway Mahaffey. I am thankful to my sister–cousin, Cynithea Reeder, for her ability to capture the theme of this book's contents in her artistic rendering depicted on the cover of this book. I am thankful to my aunts, uncles, cousins, friends, and mentors who have been supportive of this scholarly effort. Most importantly, I am eternally grateful to The Creator, without whom, none of this would be possible.

Contents

Concrete Examples

Advancing the National Conversation on Race Among Churches of Christ

Introduction

by Tanya Smith Brice

CONTEMPORARY CHURCHES OF CHRIST IN AMERICA ARE ROOTED in the Restoration Movement of the early 1800s, often referred to as the Stone-Campbell Movement. It began as an attempt to return to the church of the New Testament in its governance, doctrine, and worship style, and was intended to be a movement that unites all Christians. Over time however, the movement has been characterized by separation and division. There are three main branches of this movement in the United States: the Christian Church/ Churches of the Christ (instrumental), the Disciples of Christ, and Churches of Christ.[1] Within the Churches of Christ, there are six identified branches: (1) Mainline; (2) Non-cooperatives; (3) One-cuppers; (4) Pre-millennial; (5) Non Sunday School; and, (6) Black Churches of Christ.[2] The identification of one division within the Churches of Christ as "Black Churches of Christ" indicates that racial division is a major issue within this fellowship. This division is most pronounced when the Churches of Christ is placed within the context of American history.

The Church of Christ in Black and White

Members of the Church of Christ, particularly in slaveholding states, broadly supported the institution of slavery, and were often slaveholders. The following account provides a glimpse of the relationship between the slaveholder and the enslaved within the context of an early congregation:

> In these early days slaves drove their masters to the services, others living near came and stood on the outside while several went in to assist with the children or to do any other kind of work assigned. Some of the slaves being deeply impressed, sought spiritual guidance. They were already in Hades and to hear a man of God tell them how they might secure peace and sit down at the welcome table pleased them very much. They did not choose to go to a torment greater than the one already experienced. It had been hard to understand the preaching, but now this simple way of telling the old, old story appealed to most of them. Several were added to the church. Often these went back and told the news to the other slaves. Many believed and were baptized; others were taught by the masters and their families. At times the most gifted among the slaves were trained and allowed to preach to the rest. Occasionally slaves were gathered in separate buildings and were preached to by the evangelists either before or after the regular service.[3]

Many in this period did not see a conflict between their desire to follow Jesus' teachings, the growth of the church, and the institution of slavery. Slaveholders often planted churches for the enslaved. It was not uncommon to hear the myths of the Curse of Ham and the Curse of Cain preached from the pulpit to justify slavery as part of God's plan and desire.[4] These myths have lasting effects on contemporary race relations in the church.

The institution of chattel slavery was later replaced with a system of apartheid, commonly referred to as the era of Jim Crow. Many leaders of the Churches of Christ fought diligently to justify and maintain this system. God and the Bible were often employed as instruments of social control and social alienation. For instance, Alexander Bigby Lipscomb (1876–1940), nephew of David Lipscomb, provided interesting insight into the "remarkable success" of black leader Marshall Keeble (1878–1968), often cited as one of the most successful evangelists among Churches of Christ. Lipscomb observed, after a campaign led by Keeble in Valdosta, Georgia, had resulted in more than 329 baptisms of both blacks and whites. He noted:

> Such preaching has not only created a new religious and moral status for the Negro element, but it has brought to this community a new citizenry capable of thinking in terms of the Bible. This means that we now have better farm hands, better porters, better cooks, better housemaids than ever before.[5]

It is clear from the younger Lipscomb's assessment that the value of conversion and planting churches for the formerly enslaved is found in creating a better quality class of servants. "In countless other home fields where the Negroes flourish and need to be taught," he suggested that this "method should be replicated."

> Is it not fitting that the descendants of the race whom our fathers kept in the bondage of human slavery but to whom civilization brought the gift of emancipation, should now be led by the white children of the present generation out of the darkness and bondage of sin into "the glorious libcity [sic] of the children of God"?[6]

While the younger Lipscomb saw the work of Keeble as "remarkable," he never considered Keeble or any other African American as his equal. He saw it as the duty of "the white children of the present generation" to lead the "descendants of the race whom [his] fathers kept in the bondage of human slavery" to salvation. Unfortunately, Lipscomb's comments were not uncommon among leaders in the Churches of Christ.

As the United States continued to struggle with an ever changing society where descendants of the enslaved applied increasing pressure for civil rights, many leaders of the Church of Christ resisted this pressure. At a 1963 lectureship held at the Florida Christian College, Franklin Puckett, a Church of Christ preacher of Dyersburg, Tennessee, delivered a lecture entitled, "The Messiah and Racial Problems." Puckett admits to approaching the subject of race relations with "fear and trembling."

> So many people have fixed opinions on the race question and deliberately close their minds and hearts to any delineation of facts or presentation of arguments which do not harmonize with those opinions. Emotionalism often shuts out realism, and sectional bias frequently closes the door on factual truth. Because of these factors, it is easy for one to be misunderstood. For these reasons I have written out what I want to say on this subject, so that I, at least, will know what I have said.[7]

In laying the foundation for his view of race relations, Puckett assured his audience that his argument was based on "factual truth." He then explains,

> Notwithstanding the equality of the relation and service in the spiritual realm, there is another principle revealed in the teaching of the Messiah that must be recognized and respected. The practice of righteousness does not require, as some have erroneously concluded, the abolition of social and political distinctions in the civil realm. . . . There have always been—and always will be—social distinctions in the civil realm which do not exist in the spiritual; nor is their existence out of harmony with New Testament Christianity. A failure to recognize this truth is responsible for much of the confusion relative to racial problems. . . . Let each remain in his own state without being concerned over external matters, but rather concern himself with the doing of God's will. . . . Let every man abide in the calling wherein he was called. If both the whites and the blacks would practice this instruction, they would be unconcerned about the color of their skin or the changing of the external customs

stemming therefrom; instead they would be devoted to the practice of the will of God within their respective spheres.[8]

Puckett compares the "social and political distinctions in the civil realm" to marital and parenting relationships, in that there are agreed upon roles that exist because that is the way that God intended. He suggests that Christians should not be concerned with social injustices like the Jim Crow policies of that era, but with God's will, as if these are competing concerns.

These sentiments are not atypical of Southern, white preachers in the Churches of Christ during this era. In a 1954 essay entitled, "Segregation or Christianity," Bryan Vinson, a well-respected preacher in the Churches of Christ, argued against the notion that segregation and Christianity cannot coexist. His essay, published five months after the Brown v. Board of Education landmark ruling that had declared segregation of public schools unconstitutional, expressed his views concerning desegregation of public schools in general, and the desegregation of private, Christian schools specifically.

> First, Christianity is dependent for its current and practical existence among us on two external influences: (1) The decision of the Supreme Court recently holding segregation in public schools to be unconstitutional. Just think of the five previous decisions to the contrary which obstructed the inauguration and practice of the (whole) principle of Christianity. Christianity is here made to depend on the point of constitutionality as established by a political court, rather than on scripturality as established by the Word of God! Amazing in its absurdity! (2) With respect to admission of Negroes into "Christian Schools," it is pointed out that we have the very splendid example of denominational institutions bravely doing this even before the recent decision of the Court. Hence, we gain support from this source as an example worthy to follow. It has been long my persuasion that when brethren make appeals in behalf of anything and are given to citing denominational procedure as precedents for such that the proposal merits suspicion.[9]

Vinson, then compared equality of the races with the equality of the sexes:

> One could conclude that since "as many of you as have been
> baptized into Christ have put on Christ. There is neither Jew nor
> Greek, there is neither bond nor free, there is neither male nor
> female, for ye are all one in Christ Jesus" that no distinction or
> segregation of the sexes can be practiced. Hence, if the equal-
> ity pleaded for . . . be founded on this passage and involves the
> mixing of the negro with the whites in dormitories, it would
> also require the mixing of the males and females, or else there
> would be discrimination. This passage has nothing to do with
> social equality, but simply teaches that which all recognize as
> true; namely, that all men need salvation, and God has one plan
> to save all.

Vinson here made the distinction between equality in Christ and social
equality among the races, agreeing in concept with Puckett's civil realm
versus a spiritual realm distinction. Vinson, however, pressed his logic further and reflected the attitude of many white Southerners of his era:

> The question before us in this hour is not Segregation or
> Christianity, but rather it is Segregation or Miscegenation.
> Within a very few generations of non-segregation there shall
> be inevitably a widespread mixing and mongrelizing of the
> two races by intermarriage. . . . Place the two races together on
> every plane of social intercourse, in the schools, the churches,
> the parks, the swimming pools and the social parlor and these
> developments shall follow. . . . In the same vein, I think we
> should remain unaffected by what the denominations are doing
> about segregation, and strive to promote and safeguard the
> interests of both races by maintaining that separateness which is
> best for all. While it is true that "what God has joined together
> let no man put asunder," equally true, in principle, is it that what
> God has separated let not man put together.

Vinson suggests in this same essay that miscegenation is "playing into the hands of Communist propaganda and design" and identifies with "'one world' idea of internationalism." In a later essay, Vinson wrote that he "believe[d] in the relative superiority and inferiority, respectively, of the white and black races . . . the amalgamation, blending, and miscegenation of the two will mark the utter ruin of this nation . . . moral, economic, social, intellectual, and . . . national and international consequences ensuing in wholly irrepairable[sic] harm."[10] In this way, Vinson freely identified with a white supremacy ideology. "Why have I written as I have done?" Vinson asked his readers, "primarily, in response to a provocation wrought by the charge that I am a White Supremist. This is one thing with which I have been charged, to which I plead guilty."[11] While these examples may seem shocking in today's context, the historical record is replete with examples of this kind of attitude among leaders in the Churches of Christ.[12]

Oneness in Christ?

There were those among the leadership of Churches of Christ who openly confronted these racist views. David Lipscomb (1831–1917), an influential leader in the Restoration movement and editor of *The Gospel Advocate*, often expressed his views against white supremacy in the church. In 1878, in response to overt objections to an African American man seeking membership in a white Texas congregation, Lipscomb suggested that racially segregated congregations were sinful. Drawing on the multicultural composition of the early church and their struggle with racial prejudices, he noted:

> The race prejudice was as strong with them as with us. Did Christ or the Holy Spirit tolerate those who objected to association with the Gentiles who believed? Not once. All were accepted by Christ as brethren, and were required so to live. There was nothing of having two congregations in the same community for the distinct races. Such a course would have defeated the very ends of Christ's mission, to make of twain, one new man. So make peace.[13]

Lipscomb acknowledged that racism was a societal issue that has been present throughout history. However, he made the argument that Christians were to be countercultural, and he applied that principle to the church of his day when he wrote the following:

> We believe it is sinful to have two congregations in the same community for persons of separate and distinct races now. The race prejudice would cause trouble in the churches we know. It did this in apostolic days. Not once did the apostles suggest that they should form separate congregations for the different races. But they always admonished them to unity, forbearance, love and brotherhood in Christ Jesus. . . . For the Whites to reject the Negro is to make the whites self-righteous, self-sufficient, exclusive and unchristian in spirit.[14]

Other voices took a softer tone, than Lipscomb, in admonishing church leaders against white supremacy ideology. In a 1970 essay, Forrest D. Moyer, a preacher from California and Texas, delineated, with explanation, what Christians should do: "Preach the gospel to those of any nation" and "A Christian will not refuse to eat with one of a different nation". He ends the essay with a very interesting thought. After quoting James 3:8–10, Moyer posits:

> This ought to impress upon us the fact that we must treat all men with proper respect. All men are just a little lower than the angels. We cannot put ourselves on a pedestal above those of another race. This does not mean that I am advocating for inter-marriage between the white and negro: I am not [author's emphasis]. But I am advocating that we treat all mankind with the respect that our Father desires that we have. Therefore, let us seek to teach truth to all people. Let us bring them to hear the truth. We dare not withhold the gospel.[15]

While Moyer chastised his white brethren for racial favoritism, he negated this chastisement with one sentence: "This does not mean that I am advocating for inter-marriage between the white and negro." This is followed by a very clear "I am not." Moyer seemed ambivalent about how far one should carry the principles of favoritism and oneness in Christ. While he believed that there should be fellowship with African Americans, he is clearly against miscegenation between the races, which is a hallmark of white supremacist ideology.

The tumultuous era known as the Civil Rights era proved to be a challenging time for the church, and leaders often found themselves holding a position of general indifference. Distinguished historian Leroy Garrett (1919–2015) has well noted that most members of white Churches of Christ preferred the attitude of Georgia's Governor Maddox, "who as a business man closed his restaurant rather than serve food to a Negro" rather than Mayor Lindsey of New York "who helped to avoid riots in his city by joining hands with Negro mourners and singing "We Shall Overcome." "We are, for the most part, a southern church," Garrett lamented, "and yet our witness for Christ in reference to the cause of the deprived Negro is virtually nil."[16]

However broader social and cultural traditions also influenced black Churches of Christ as well. They remained reluctant to participate in the Civil Rights movement largely because it was led by a Baptist minister. Having been taught to operate in the same "spiritual realm" as described by Puckett, and not in the "civil realm," despite the direct impact the civil rights movement had on their status in this country. Ironically, one of the lesser known leaders in the Civil Rights movement was Fred Gray, Dr. Martin Luther King Jr's Alabama attorney. Gray, a student of Keeble's Nashville Christian Institute, is a minister in the Church of Christ. Gray played a significant role in the Civil Rights movement, challenging the legality of America's apartheid policies.[17] Gray has recounted his experience with Marshall Keeble in this way:

> Even Brother Marshall Keeble, the great pioneer preacher who
> had carried me, as a boy preacher, around with him representing
> the Nashville Christian Institute, probably did not understand
> my position. One preacher who had been a student at NCI when
> I was there later said to Brother Keeble about me, "Fred Gray is

smart. He is involved in the Civil Rights Movement." Brother Keeble is reported to have replied, "He's too smart." I could understand Brother Keeble's position. A portion of his preaching and work in the church had been sponsored by white members of the Church of Christ. I am quite confident that it was difficult for him to understand how one of his former boy preachers would now be standing in courtrooms fighting against racial discrimination.[18]

There appeared to be a conflict between Gray's vocation as a preacher in the Church of Christ, and as an attorney, particularly in the Civil Rights movement. However, Gray balanced the perceived conflict, stating, "While I recognized it would be a tremendous responsibility for me to carry on a full-time law practice—particularly the demanding civil rights cases—and to serve as full time minister, I saw no conflict between the two."[19] Gray was able to operate in both the spiritual and civil realms.

Advancing the National Conversation on Race

There have been several efforts to advance the national conversation on race among the Churches of Christ. There were conferences on race in 1968 and 1998 among Church of Christ ministers and church leaders. The national conversation has regained momentum over the past several years. There is a National Strategic Planning Team of ministers and church leaders who have met over the past several years to develop a strategy for advancing this conversation. As a result of that initiative, Racial Unity Leadership Summits, led by members of the National Strategic Planning Team, have taken place in several communities across the country. These summits bring together Church of Christ leaders to discuss race issues in their community. The Christian Scholars Conference is a national conference that seeks "to create and nurture an intellectual and Christian community that joins individuals and institutions to stimulate networks of scholarly dialogue and collaboration." This annual conference has several research sections, one of which is the Civil Rights section. This book, conceived as an output of the National Strategic Planning Team, includes essays originally presented in the Civil Rights section of the Christian Scholars Conference and as part of the Racial Unity Leadership Summits.

This collection of essays seeks to provide an opportunity for truth telling with the goal of seeking out racial reconciliation. It is my prayer that this collection will be used in small discussion groups. Each essay is followed with a set of discussion questions with a goal of advancing a national conversation among our fellowship.

We begin with an examination of our historical realities as a fellowship.

- **Brad McKinnon's essay** examines social ethics in the Churches of Christ through the lens of *Mission*, a journal published within our fellowship from 1967–1987. *Mission* focused on race relations, as well as other social issues, in ways that other Church of Christ periodicals did not. McKinnon evaluates Mission's effectiveness in addressing race relations within a larger societal and ecclesiastical context.
- **Yukikazu Obata's essay** examines the missionary efforts of J.M. McCaleb, a missionary to Japan, who many consider to be the father of missions among Churches of Christ. Obata suggests that McCaleb's racist attitudes towards Blacks in the United States influenced his work in Japan.
- **Doug Foster's essay** documents the solidified estrangement between black and white Churches of Christ in the racially charged events of 1967 and 1968 across the United States which directly impacted race relations between black and white congregations across the country.
- **Mark Tucker's essay** describes the role that members of the Churches of Christ played in the integration of Little Rock, Arkansas' Central High School. He highlights a missed opportunity by leaders of local Churches of Christ to lead reconciliation efforts in Little Rock.
- **Richard Hughes' essay** rounds out this section with his reflections on the failure of the white Churches of Christ to embrace racial equality, particularly during the Civil Rights Movement.

The next section engages in truth telling about the contemporary challenges to race relations among Churches of Christ.

- **Stanley Tolbert** challenges us to use radical love, as patterned by Jesus Christ, to engage in racial reconciliation as individuals, as neighbors, and in a sociopolitical context. Tolbert uses the context of the racial turmoil of Ferguson, Missouri, and the rise of Black Lives Matter movement to make sense of radical love.
- **Lawrence Rogers** challenges us to speak out about racism and other social injustices. He recounts recent events such as the racist attack on the Bible study class at Emmanuel AME in Charleston, South Carolina, the social unrest in Baltimore, Maryland, and the countless other instances of injustice experienced in this nation. Rogers suggests that churches in our fellowship must be vocal in denouncing the sin of racism.
- **Jerry Taylor** shares a sermon where he admonishes us to not be influenced by the racism institutionalized in our society. Taylor provides biblical examples of Jesus modeling for us how to interact across racial lines in a way that challenges status quo.

The final section of essays give concrete examples of how leaders within local congregations can engage in racial reconciliation within our fellowship.

- **William Turner's essay** describes the challenges of interracial communication. Specifically, Turner introduces microaggressions as a phenomenon that often occur when people with social differences, such as race or gender, interact. He encourages the reader to be mindful of ways in which they may engage in microaggressive behaviors.
- **David Fleer's sermon** furthers the discussion by encouraging the reader to take ownership in their own racist behaviors. He calls us to action as we reconsider reconciliation.
- **Don McLaughlin's essay** provides tangible examples of how a congregation of the Churches of Christ can strive towards racial reconciliation. The essay describes the multi-racial congregation,

in the Deep South, for which McLaughlin pastors. He provides context for and strategies to help congregations struggle through this process.

- This collection of essays concludes with **Phyllis Hildreth's suggestions** for ways in which congregations can manage the conflict that inevitably arises in reconciliation work. Hildreth provides relevant resources for the reader to assist in the reconciliation process.

Reconciliation takes time. It will not happen in a quick fashion. Most importantly, it cannot happen without Christ. This process must include the study of Christ's teachings as a fundamental component. It will require a great deal of spiritual discipline. Reconciliation will seem like an impossible task to most. However, we must be reminded of Jesus' words as recorded in Matthew 19:26, "With man this is impossible, but with God all things are possible."

Notes

[1] Foster, Douglas A., Paul M. Blowers, Anthony L. Dunnavant, and D. Newell Williams ed., *The Encyclopedia of the Stone-Campbell Movement*. (Grand Rapids: MI, Wm. B. Eerdmans Publishing Co., 2005.

[2] Leroy Garrett, *The History of the Stone-Campbell Movement* (Joplin, MO: The College Press, 1981).

[3] Alfred J. DeGroot and Winfred E. Garrison, *The Disciples of Christ* (St. Louis: The Bethany Press 1948), 469.

[4] Edward Robinson, *The Fight is On in Texas* (Abilene, TX: Abilene Christian University Press, 2008). Also, see David M. Goldenberg. *The Curse of Ham* (Princeton, N.J.: Princeton University Press), 2003; and, Regina M. Schwartz, *The Curse of Cain: The Violent Legacy of Monotheism* (Chicago: University of Chicago Press, 1997) for more discussion of these two philosophies and their influence on race relations.

[5] A.B. Lipscomb, "It's Not Keeble, But the Bible is Right," *Christian Leader* 45 (August 25 1931), 6.

[6] Ibid

[7] Franklin Puckett, "The Messiah and Racial Problems," *Truth Magazine* 7,8 (1963): 11–20.

[8] Ibid.

[9] Bryan Vinson, "Segregation or Christianity,"*Gospel Guardian* 6,2 (October 1954): 8–9.

[10] Bryan Vinson, *Gospel Guardian* 23, pp. 19–20, as quoted in Jeffery Kingry, "The Christian and Race Relations", *The Truth Magazine* 21,34 (1977): 536–539.

[11] Ibid.

[12] See Don Haymes, "Race and the Church of Christ," which is a collection of primary documents chronicling members of the Church Christ's struggle with race relations dating as early as 1904. accessed March 28, 2016, https://webfiles.acu.edu/departments /Library/HR/restmov_nov11/www.mun.ca/rels/restmov/subs/race.html.

[13] David Lipscomb, "Race Prejudice", *Gospel Advocate* 20 (February 21, 1878): 120–121, as reprinted in *Gospel Guardian* 22,2 (May 14, 1970): 1–3.

[14] Ibid.

[15] Forrest Darrell Moyer, "Respect of Persons," *Gospel Guardian* 22, 3 (1970): 5.

[16] Leroy Garrett, "Martin Luther King, Jr.: A symbol of peace or violence?" *Restoration Review*, Vol. 10, No. 5, 1968.

[17] Fred D. Gray, *Bus Ride to Justice: Changing the System by the System: The Life and Works of Fred D. Gray, Preacher, Attorney, Politician* (Montgomery, AL: NewSouth Books) 2002.

[18] Ibid, 257.

[19] Ibid, 257.

HISTORICAL
REALITIES

1968 and the Reshaping of the Separation Between Black and White Churches of Christ

by Douglas A. Foster

The Larger Context of 1968

ON FEBRUARY 8TH, 1968, THE THIRD NIGHT OF A PEACEFUL PROTEST staged largely by students from the historic black South Carolina State University at a whites-only bowling alley in Orangeburg, state troopers with shotguns opened fire on the protesters. Three teenage college students were killed, and twenty-seven injured, many seriously.[1]

The next month, students at the renowned black Howard University in Washington, DC staged a five-day sit-in, laying siege to the administration building and shutting down the university. Reflecting the sentiments on campuses across the country, the Howard students were protesting the school's ROTC program that supplied a stream of young men for service in the Vietnam War. They also demanded, among other things, a new curriculum more relevant to black history and culture.[2]

Twelve days later, on April 4th, Martin Luther King, Jr. was shot and killed at the Lorraine Motel in Memphis, Tennessee. Two days later, Eldridge Cleaver and fourteen members of the Black Panther Party for

29

Self-Defense were involved in a shootout with Oakland, California police that left three officers and two Panthers wounded. Later that night Oakland police retaliated by attacking a house where Black Panthers were staying. Though the leaders in the house surrendered and were taken into custody, officers pushed sixteen-year old Bobby Hutton into the street then shot him twelve times.[3]

In July 1968, black militants led by Fred Evans engaged in a fierce three-day gunfight with police in the Glenville neighborhood of Cleveland, Ohio. After the all-white National Guard had "restored order," seven lay dead, including three police officers and three militants, with many others injured.[4]

In many ways, 1968 was the pinnacle of racial violence during the Civil Rights movement. A clear shift was taking place among black leaders. The peaceful resistance of Martin Luther King, Jr. was increasingly being replaced by calls for an active defense against white violence and denial of rights from voices like Stokely Carmichael. These five incidents are merely a sampling of the events that spotlighted the vast divide between whites and blacks in the United States reflecting the ideology of white supremacy that was so insidiously entrenched and destructive in the country.

This was the context for what happened in Churches of Christ in 1968. Churches of Christ reflected, as they always have, the larger culture, including their responses to these events. Many believed these events were a threat to the very survival of the nation. A handful of black and white leaders in these churches began to ask how they could respond in a way that might begin the healing of the divisions so deeply embedded in the fabric of the nation, and the church.

Four significant events that year provide essential insights into the matter of race relations in Churches of Christ in the Civil Rights era, with profound implications for Churches of Christ today: the Race Relations Workshop at the Schrader Lane Church of Christ in Nashville, Tennessee, March 4 to 8; the Atlanta Race Relations Workshop, June 25 and 26; the July issue of *20th Century Christian* magazine titled, "Christ and Race Relations"; and a series of four radio broadcasts by Herald of Truth the same month dealing explicitly with race for the first time in the ministry's history.

Schrader Lane Race Relations Workshop

From March 4–8th, the Schrader Lane Church of Christ in Nashville, Tennessee, a predominantly black congregation, hosted a race relations workshop aimed at black and white members of Churches of Christ in Middle Tennessee. The church's minister, Dr. David Jones, and others had become convinced, in light of the frightening rise in racial violence, that it was imperative to come together to respond as Christians. Unlike a small invitation-only meeting held in Nashville two years earlier,[5] organizers publicized the meeting to every Church of Christ in Nashville/ Davidson County and urged all concerned Christians to participate.

The *Christian Chronicle* published a special issue dated May 10 that included the texts of all eleven speeches as well as background material to the meeting, lists of suggested actions, and photographs of those attending.[6] In the opening message, David Jones noted the rising disgust of young Christians with the hypocrisy with which the church had dealt with the "race problem." As an illustration, he recounted a recent incident in which a white minister from Churches of Christ stood and announced in an all-white neighborhood meeting that favored Negros moving in, that he was leading a group opposing such a move. When such a thing can happen, Jones insisted, "we need to be here."

In his final argument for this race relations meeting, Jones noted the serious need for white Christians to become aware of the deep psychological and sociological damage paternalism had inflicted on blacks. Whites almost universally assumed a benevolent (and superior) attitude toward their black sisters and brothers, providing church buildings and giving song books, Bibles, etc. Such actions made the whites feel good and removed any reason to treat their black sisters and brothers as equals in the full Christian sense. However, these white donations were all too often items ready to be discarded from use and in poor condition. Though black leaders gave warm smiles and received such benevolent gifts with open arms, in actuality, they tucked these substandard donations away into forgotten corners. Pulling no punches, Jones accused the black church—especially the preachers—of perpetuating "the subservient position of the Negro because the white Church and its conscience-soothing gifts represented its meal ticket."[7]

Jones boldly exposed the fact that white Christians had no concept of the damage done by, or even the reality of, the systemic and consistent discrimination—even if "benevolent"—that was behind the rising black rage so incomprehensible to white members of Churches of Christ. "I don't think we really know each other," he said. "By this, I mean we're not really aware of the feelings, attitudes, habits, and customs of the other group. We only have notions about what we're supposed to be like and how we're supposed to act while around each other."[8]

The second message was by white Nashville businessman Lawrence L. (Bud) Stumbaugh, who delivered perhaps the most biting of all the presentations. He warned the audience that he was "going to inflict some red-hot realism" upon them. "I intend to raise a howl of calamity about the past, present, and persistent failure of the church to be what it ought to be." "The problem of the nation," he continued, "Cannot be properly labeled the Negro Problem. It was and always had been a white problem."[9]

Stumbaugh recounted the horrors of slavery and the white Christian rationalization of the institution. He exposed the absurdity of whites blaming blacks for the current unrest in the nation as comparable to accusing a doctor who diagnoses a patient's cancer of causing the cancer. "The black man was blinded by the white man, so to speak, and then condemned for not being able to see. The very people who had amputated his legs were now criticizing him for being a cripple." Stumbaugh had begun his speech with the frank confession that what bothered his conscience most deeply was "the realization that one does not have to be grossly wicked to be immoral, just spineless." He closed with an endorsement of "black power," and urged black Christians to use black power "more humanely and morally" than whites had used the white power they had exercised for so long.[10]

Three other major addresses and six shorter statements by college students were surrounded by question and answer sessions. The *Christian Chronicle* reported that attendance at the five-night workshop ranged from 357 on the first night, to a high of 708. While the ratio of blacks and whites was roughly equal at least one night, most audiences were majority black.[11] And despite the strong, clear and inspiring messages and discussion, little seemed to change.

Atlanta Race Relations Workshop

The second event was the Atlanta Race Relations Workshop held at the Hilton Hotel at Hapeville, Georgia, June 25–26. This was an invitation-only meeting that included over forty leaders in black and white Churches of Christ. Behind the scenes were white evangelists John Allen Chalk, Walter Burch and Dwain Evans, who had been involved in other gatherings on race relations including the Nashville meeting in 1966, but were deemed too controversial to be the "up-front" leaders of this meeting. Respected ministers Eugene Lawton of Newark, New Jersey; R. C. Wells of the Harlem Church of Christ in New York; and Jimmy Allen of Searcy, Arkansas chaired the meeting.[12] White attendees included college Presidents John Stevens (ACU) and Clifton Ganus (Harding), publishers Jim Bill McInteer (*20th Century Christian*) and Ralph Sweet (Sweet Publishing), as well as leaders of Herald of Truth John Allen Chalk, James W. Nichols, and Highland Church of Christ elder Art Haddox. Among black leaders were widely respected ministers Franklin D. Florence, Humphrey Foutz, Andrew J. Hairston, R. N. Hogan, G. P. Holt, David Jones, and Orum Lee Trone, Sr.[13]

Andrew Hairston, minister for the Simpson Street Church of Christ and widely respected Atlanta lawyer and judge, spoke first on "Spiritual Equality in Christ." He insisted that Christians must regard racial segregation as sin and must regard every person as a whole being. Abilene Christian College faculty member Carl Spain followed, denouncing racial discrimination as evil. He struck at the way white Churches of Christ interpreted scripture, seen in the utter failure to understand the nature of the inclusivity of Christ's Church. "Our basic sin is lying in the handling of the Bible. We have mishandled the word of God." "We were taught wrong," he exclaimed.[14]

The group met for two days, and at the end of the workshop they produced a document that acknowledged the sin of racial prejudice widespread throughout Churches of Christ. The document proposed a list of actions designed to help end "discrimination in all of its forms in the life of the church." The document included proposals for local churches, church-related institutions (colleges), the Herald of Truth, publishing companies and Christian bookstores, Christian-owned businesses, and for all individual Christians. Proposals included integrating congregations;

increasing the number of black students, faculty and trustees at Christian colleges; speaking against racism on Herald of Truth and using black speakers for the radio and television broadcasts; publishing materials by black leaders; and hiring blacks for "front-office" jobs and managerial positions. This list was published in several media outlets, including *Mission Journal* and the *Christian Chronicle*.[15]

Five white attendees did not sign the document, notably the two college presidents and the two publishers present (though Sweet later indicated he was greatly impacted by the meeting).[16] Yet many had great hope for change as a result of the Schrader Lane and Atlanta meetings and the recommendations that emerged from them. Two areas that began immediate action in response to the recommendations were 20th Century Christian Publishing Company and Herald of Truth.

20th *Century Christian* July 1968: "Christ and Race Relations"

The third event was already under way at the time of the Atlanta Race Relations Workshop but was a concrete example of the meeting's recommendation to "Publish more articles on the issue of racial discrimination and injustices."[17] The July 1968 issue of *20th Century Christian* magazine was titled "Christ and Race Relations," and was co-edited by Bill Banowsky, then minister of the Broadway Church of Christ in Lubbock, Texas, and a *20th Century Christian* editor; and Clyde Muse, long-time minister in Oklahoma City. Authors were balanced equally between black and white leaders. Among the titles of white-written articles were "It is Time to Confess our Sins" (Jennings Davis, Jr.), "Tear Down the Walls" (Matt Young), and "Total Equality in Christ" (John Allen Chalk). Black writers wrote "The Contradiction of Racist Christianity" (R. C. Wells), "Black Power? White Power?" (Eugene Lawton), and "Tokenism Versus Meaningful Integration" (Humphrey Foutz).

The response from the magazine's readership was mixed at best. According to one source, the circulation of *20th Century Christian* dropped by half after the publication of the issue on race, from 40,000 to 20,000.[18] Even in the bold and clear identification of racism, segregation and white supremacy as sin, and the hope such public statements engendered, the frustration of both white activists and black members of Churches of Christ was growing.

Herald of Truth Radio Sermons on Race

The final event also took place soon after the Atlanta meeting. John Allen Chalk, then radio speaker for the Herald of Truth, the only national broadcast ministry of Churches of Christ, wrote and delivered four radio sermons addressing racism. Three proposals from the Atlanta race relations workshop were specifically aimed at the ministry: speak courageously on the sin of racial discrimination on both radio and TV; use blacks in TV film series in various roles, not simply subservient roles; and use black speakers on radio and TV in the course of a year. These broadcasts, however, were already on the drawing board before the Atlanta meeting occurred.

The messages were titled: "Hatred is only Skin Deep," "Is Jehovah God a Racist?" "Are You a Respecter of Persons?" and "Some of My Best Friends."[19] Drawing from sources like the *Report of the National Advisory Commission on Civil Disorders*, Swedish scholar Gunnar Myrdal's study *An American Dilemma: The Negro Problem and Modern Democracy*, and *The Autobiography of Malcolm X*, Chalk took aim at white racism in America and in the American church. The message was clear and concise: "Where racism flourishes Christianity dies. And where Christ rules the hearts and lives of men, racism is destroyed. But the Christianity that destroys racism will not be the weak, watered-down, reshaped caricature of Christianity that flourishes today."[20]

Letters in reaction to Chalk's lessons soon began to arrive at Herald of Truth offices in Abilene. While some were favorable, many regarded such messages as a betrayal of Herald of Truth's mandate to be a strictly evangelistic ministry. One correspondent wrote, "Dear Brother Chalk, I am writing to express displeasure with your sermons on racism. I am white, but not prejudice [sic] against any race, but I think your preaching is toward the extreme. I noticed two Sundays ago that half your sermon was preached before I heard one passage of scripture quoted. . . . Brother Chalk, if you preach the word, . . . people will become Christians, and race problems vanish at that point. You are working on the wrong end."[21]

After the message on July 21 titled "Are You a Respecter of Persons?" Chalk received a letter from Odessa, Texas. "Dear sir, heard your radio broadcast Sunday 7-21-68, re —INTERROGATION & INTERBREEDING OF THE RACES. I disagree with you. Besides, in the pulpit, you should be preaching for the purpose of saving lost souls. My, how we do need this purpose propagated. . . . Seems to me that GOD himself separated and segregated the races—The black people in Africa, The whites in the West and The Orientals in the East. But now you and Martin Luther King have a better idea."[22]

Other letters were more overtly offensive, referring to blacks as thieves, liars, and wild animals, and accusing the Civil Rights movement of having an agenda not of "a colored child in every school room but a colored man in every bed room." Some threatened to cut off support if such preaching continued. That threat began to materialize in October when the White Avenue Church of Christ in Henderson, Tennessee wrote saying that since there had been no "change in the direction of the program, we are not planning to include Herald of Truth in our budget next year."[23]

The letters reflected a deeply held theological idea that reflected what many believed was the American ideal of separation of church and state. The idea, however, had taken on a particularly insidious form when paired with the Christian defense of slavery, and later the systemic creation by white Christians of a new and comprehensive system of separation and subordination of black citizens. The church's task, the idea went, is to spread the pure Gospel, and not to become enmeshed in political and social campaigns that distract from and pervert the pure Gospel. Charles Reagan Wilson in his study *Baptized in Blood: The Religion of the Lost Cause 1885–1928* detailed the development of the doctrine that led white churches, particularly in the South but ultimately nationwide, to see themselves as "custodians of unadulterated evangelism and instruments to develop pure Christian civilization."[24]

A classic statement of this doctrine held by white members of Churches of Christ appeared in the *Firm Foundation* of March 31, 1964. Christians before the Civil War, author James Fowler asserted, "did not turn from their primary purpose of preaching Christ to become involved in revolutionary demands and social reforms." In the early church, he continued, the apostles never tried to disrupt "the legal, social system that prevailed, and they did not make the church party to political movements and pressure groups." Christians who became involved with efforts like the Civil Rights movement were in fact acting contrary to the spirit of Christianity and true justice.[25]

This, of course, was the white view. Black members of Churches of Christ had a different vision of the pure gospel. The events we have surveyed had engendered hope in the hearts of many black members of Churches of Christ that true change was underway. Those hopes were largely eroded when blacks witnessed the fearful and angry responses of many whites in Churches of Christ, and the indifference of even more. One year before the Schrader Lane Race Relations Workshop, a profoundly insightful article by editor Harold Straughn had appeared in the March 8, 1967 issue of the *Christian Chronicle*. Titled "New Negro Era Begins at Southwestern." The article included parts of an interview with Dr. Jack Evans, who had recently become president of Southwestern Christian College in Terrell, Texas, the only historic black college in Churches of Christ.

The term "new Negro" had been used in the 1920s to refer to a new hope and strength among African American communities in several US cities that developed vibrant subcultures of art, education, publishing, film, and business. "New Negro" contrasted with the stereotypical image of the subservient, ineffectual black created during four hundred years of oppression in America. Straughn used the term as symbolic of the coming of Jack Evans as the first black president of Southwestern. Impressive strides had already been made under Evans' leadership, including new science labs, music classrooms, creation of a ten-year campus development plan and a drive for accreditation. The lack of planning by the previous white leadership had led the college to near collapse, Straughn said. But now, under black leadership the school had a bright future. "There is a new Negro in the church today. The 'new Negro' differs from the older Negro generation in his determination to practice New Testament Christianity without dependence on white support."[26]

Evans reminded readers of the recent closing of another black educational institution, Nashville Christian Institute, with its half million-dollar endowment given to David Lipscomb College. In the minds and the hearts of black members of Churches of Christ that event represented one more indignity by whites—the takeover of a school to which they had given their blood, sweat, tears, and money, which had been sold and the money given to an institution that had barred them from attending during most of its existence, until forced to by the federal government. The article then closed with a statement that would become the reality of the relationship between black and white Churches of Christ largely to this day. "The court action [regarding the closing of Nashville Christian Institute] was one of the first signs that many of the 100,000 people who make up a Negro brotherhood, separated from the white brotherhood by scars far deeper than the railroad tracks in Terrell, Texas, are ready to exchange servility and dependence for independence, and, if need be, estrangement."[27]

Black institutions were already in place: the Annual National Lectureship, the National Youth Conference, Southwestern Christian College and its annual Lectureship, and the monthly paper the *Christian Echo*. Other lectureships developed including the Southeast Lectureship of Churches of Christ begun in 1974, and the Church of Christ Ladies Lectureship-Retreat begun in 1986. Black Churches of Christ had a completely self-contained and self-sufficient network and culture.

And so, the events of 1968, rather than bringing black and white members of Churches of Christ closer together on an equal basis, instead reshaped the long-existing separation. Black churches were already moving strongly toward a rejection of the patronizing relationship white churches had maintained with black churches. It was not so much that black Christians wanted to be separate, but a resignation to the fact, reinforced by the events of 1968, that despite the hopes and even some movement toward equality and unity, whites as a whole had no desire to associate with, much less see themselves as equals to blacks, whether they were their brothers and sisters or not. With some exceptions, the estrangement is still largely in place. The failure to "know each other" identified by David Jones in March 1968 is still operative. Understanding the truth of what happened in 1968 I believe can aid in acquiring that deep spiritual knowledge of each other that has the potential with the help of God to bring repentance and unity.

Discussion Questions

1. The author describes several pivotal events that provided context for opportunities that the Churches of Christ had to respond to the civil unrest in US society in 1968. What are some pivotal events of today to which the Churches of Christ has opportunity to respond? In what ways has your congregation responded?

2. If you were to put together a gathering to discuss race relations among Churches of Christ, who would you invite?

3. Identify the black Church of Christ congregations and the white Church of Christ congregations within your community. How often do you interact with each of the other congregations in a calendar year? What is the nature of the interaction? Count the number of individuals with whom you personally interact at each of the other congregations? What is the nature of the interaction? In what ways could you improve the quality of the congregational and individual interactions?

Notes

[1] http://newsreel.org/video/SCARRED-JUSTICE-ORANGEBURG-MASSACRE-1968; Jack Bass and Jack Nelson, *The Orangeburg Massacre* (Mercer University Press, 2003).

[2] "A Glimpse of History: Scenes from the Howard University1968 Takeover," http://www.pbs.org/wgbh/pages/frontline/shows/race/etc/history.html/.

[3] Frontline Interview with Eldridge Cleaver, http://www.pbs.org/wgbh/pages/frontline/shows/race/interviews/ecleaver.html, accessed January 21, 2016.

[4] "The Glenville Shootout," The Cleveland Memory Project, at http://www.clevelandmemory.org/gville/.

[5] Richard T. Hughes and R. L. Roberts, *Churches of Christ*, Student Edition (Westport, Connecticut, 2001) 137.

[6] "Report on Race Relations Workshop," *Christian Chronicle* (May 10, 1968): 1–32; This issue of the *Christian Chronicle* is also available at http://digitalcommons.acu.edu/sc_arc_journals/16/.

[7] David Jones, Jr., "We are Deeply Honored" *Christian Chronicle* (May 10, 1968): 4.

[8] Jones, 3.

[9] Lawrence L. (Bud) Stumbaugh, "Tonight I am Going to Inflict," *Christian Chronicle* (May 10, 1968): 5.

[10] Stumbaugh, 5, 10.

[11] "Background of Race Relations Workshop," *Christian Chronicle* (May 10, 1968) 3.

[12] Don Haymes, Eugene Randall II, and Douglas A. Foster, "Race Relations," in *Encyclopedia of the Stone-Campbell Movement* (Eerdmans, 2004), 621; "Conference on Race Relations," *Mission Journal* 2 (September 1968) 24.

[13] "Conference on Race Relations," *Mission*, 25.

[14] "Atlanta Conference Studies Race," *Christian Chronicle* (July 5, 1968): 1.

[15] "Conference on Race Relations," *Mission*, pp. 24–26; "Atlanta Race Relations Conference Lists Recommendations for Improvement," *Christian Chronicle* (July 12, 1968): 4.

[16] Ralph Sweet, "You're Standing on My Boots," *Christian Chronicle* (July 5, 1968): 2.

[17] "Conference on Race Relations," *Mission*, 25.

[18] Carroll Pitts, Jr., "A Critical Study of Civil Rights Practices, Attitudes and Responsibilities in Churches of Christ" (MA Thesis, Pepperdine University, 1969) 104; Interview by Richard T. Hughes of Steven Lemley, 8 May 1994, cited in Richard T. Hughes, *The Churches of Christ* (Westport, CT: Praeger, 2001) 137, 149 footnote 47.

[19] Digital copies of the transcripts are available at the online Herald of Truth archives housed at Abilene Christian University. http://digitalcommons.acu.edu/hot/.

[20] John Allen Chalk, "Hatred is Only Skin Deep," Herald of Truth radio script 858 [July 1968].

[21] Reg Rogers, Dos Palos, CA to John Chalk, Abilene, Texas, July 15, 1968. Box 48, Race Information—Miscellaneous 1968, Herald of Truth Records, 1948–2014. Center for Restoration Studies MS# 305. Milliken Special Collections, Brown Library. Abilene Christian University, Abilene, TX.

[22] Eldon McIntosh, Odessa, Texas to Dear Sir [John Allen Chalk], Abilene, Texas, July 21, 1968. Box 48, Race Information—Miscellaneous 1968, Herald of Truth Records, 1948–2014. Center for Restoration Studies MS# 305. Milliken Special Collections, Brown Library. Abilene Christian University, Abilene, TX.

[23] Elders Church of Christ 204 White Avenue, Henderson, Tennessee to Elders, South Fifth and Highland, Abilene, Texas, October 28, 1968. Box 48, Race Information—Miscellaneous 1968, Herald of Truth Records,1948–2014. Center for Restoration Studies MS# 305. Milliken Special Collections, Brown Library. Abilene Christian University, Abilene, TX.

[24] Charles Reagan Wilson, *Baptized in Blood. The Religion of the Lost Cause: 1865–1920* (Athens, GA: The University of Georgia Press, 1980), 74, 77.

[25] James F. Fowler, "From the Midst of the Crisis," *Firm Foundation* (March 31, 1964): 199.

[26] Harold Straughn, "New Negro Era Begins at Southwestern," *Christian Chronicle* (March 8, 1967): 3.

[27] Ibid. See also, Wes Crawford, *Shattering the Illusion: How African American Churches of Christ Moved from Segregation to Independence* (Abilene Christian University Press, 2013).

The Wall that Divides

Mission and Race Relations in the Churches of Christ, 1967–1970

by Brad McKinnon

BY 1970, THERE WERE TWO MAJOR STREAMS OF THOUGHT REGARD-
ing the state of race relations within Churches of Christ. On one side,
Stanley Paregien represented a small group of dissenters who recognized
the theological significance of racism. He remarked in the February edition of Mission magazine: "Race prejudice is as thorough a denial of the
Christian God as atheism, and a far more common form of apostasy."[1] The
other stream of thought, which became the majority opinion, is represented
by Reuel Lemmons, editor of *Firm Foundation*.

In the opening of a letter written by Lemmons to John Allen Chalk,
speaker for Herald of Truth on May 16, 1968, Lemmons claimed ignorance to ongoing segregation within the Churches of Christ. Referencing an
advertisement that appeared in Firm Foundation, Lemmons saw no problem with one of the congregations participating in an evangelistic series in
San Antonio, Texas being labeled as a "negro church." Lemmons mused, "I

do not feel that any segregation was intended or implied," adding "I do not believe I have an ounce of racial prejudice in me." Lemmons went on to claim that any complaints about the language of the promotion were due to "a built-in inferiority complex." Furthermore, he considered civil rights activists to be "outside agitators bent on the disruption of societal peace." Writing six weeks after Martin Luther King Jr.'s assassination, Lemmons described King as "a modernist . . . [who] denied the faith of Jesus Christ as taught in the Bible" and as one who "advocated communistic causes." Complaining that King's faith in civil disobedience threatened the traditional Church of Christ reliance on law and order, Lemmons accused King of hypocrisy when it came to his philosophy of nonviolence: "Although King labeled himself non-violent, everything he said or did was of the nature to stir people both blacks and whites into violence." He considered King unworthy of any civic or religious praise, refusing to run a tribute to King in Firm Foundation. Don Haymes, *Mission* contributor, would later describe Lemmons' letter as "a window into the collective ambivalence of white Churches of Christ" in the late 1960s.[2]

The recipient of the correspondence, John Allen Chalk, articulated the minority view. In a *Herald of Truth* broadcast, Chalk outlined the incompatibility of racism with Christianity, emphasizing the need for believers to remain vigilant. He observed, "Where racism flourishes Christianity dies. And where Christ rules the hearts and lives of men racism is destroyed. But the Christianity that destroys racism will not be the weak, watered-down, reshaped caricature of Christianity that flourishes today."[3]

De Facto Segregation

As the more guarded Stone-Campbell fellowship, the Churches of Christ developed their identity primarily in the South between 1890 and 1940 during the nadir of race relations in the United States. While the majority of southern congregations recognized the place of Jim Crow social norms for generations, several characteristics of the Churches of Christ helped mask the divisions that existed between whites and African Americans within the religious group—including the prominence of white-operated journals, colleges, and lectureships. According to scholar Richard Hughes, these parachurch associations helped establish "an illusion of racial unity" that did not match the reality.[4]

This segregation in fact, if not by law, was most clearly demonstrated by the disparate positions of black and white southern congregations toward the struggle against Jim Crow laws during the 1950s and 1960s. Many African American Churches of Christ were involved in the Civil Rights Movement from its earliest days. While African American congregations worked cooperatively in regard to civil rights issues, the relationship with white Churches of Christ during this era was essentially non-existent.[5] Prominent white church leaders recommended gradual change. For instance, in July 1968, claiming racism was prevalent only "in an infinitesimally small part of the body of Christ," Reuel Lemmons warned that "bigotry, segregation, and prejudice must be rubbed out in the heart, rather than in the street." He concluded, "Losing sight of this could set our good efforts thus far back many years."[6] Even as late as 1990, David Jones, African American minister for the Schrader Lane congregation in Nashville, expressed disappointment regarding the state of race relations within the Churches of Christ:

> The divided relationship of the "black church of Christ" and the "white church of Christ" is as pervasive as the practice of "Jim Crow" in the southern United States prior to the late 1960s, with one exception: The church did not keep pace with the changes that took place in the legal arena of the "New South."[7]

Racial Reconciliation

Although an abolitionist presence had existed among northern Disciples of Christ before the Civil War, there was little interest among southern Churches of Christ to confront questions of race relations in the years that followed. It would be another century before serious efforts would take place among the Churches of Christ to rectify racial and social disparities within church and society. In the late 1960s, seeking to adapt to growing social pressures, some of the more progressive leaders in the Churches of Christ organized a series of workshops intended to address racial harmony within the fellowship. Under the leadership of Walter Burch (1927–2009), a church member and public relations consultant from Abilene, Texas, these integrated workshops were the first significant attempts at organized racial reconciliation among the Churches of Christ. These meetings served as a prelude to the cutting edge work of *Mission* by providing a platform for the development of a serious social ethic for the Churches of Christ in the latter half of the 20th century.

The defining meeting in this racial harmony series was held in Atlanta in late June 1968. Due primarily to the influence of *Mission*, by the time of the Atlanta meeting, the series had become a diverse effort both racially and ideologically, as it included black and white leaders that represented a theological cross-section within the Churches of Christ. The meeting concluded with the signing of a statement confessing "the sin of racial prejudice which [had] existed in Churches of Christ and church-related institutions and businesses."

While the congregational structure of Churches of Christ limited opportunities for immediate change, those sympathetic to the conference's goals saw reasons for hope. Mission described the Atlanta Conference as a meeting "intended to be [a] reasonable and realistic means to accomplish the end of discrimination in all of its forms in the life of the church." The journal called on the Churches of Christ "to hold their Christian principles and practices above the local customs of men" by "avoid[ing] the worldly attitudes and practices of racial prejudice and discrimination."[8]

Even though it did not result in any obvious visible reforms, the Atlanta Race Relations Conference was significant in two key ways. First, leadership was shared between black and white members. Previous efforts to improve race relations within the Churches of Christ tended to devolve into a white paternalistic enterprise. In this case, the integration of leadership helped to avoid defaulting into condescendence. Second, conference attendees publicly presented tangible recommendations in an attempt to address race relations within the fellowship. These proposals provided a practical framework intended to influence the approach to race relations across congregations and church-related institutions. Significantly, the conference envisioned a scope broader than American social concerns, as it recommended a reassessment of missions programs to guard against the tendency toward white paternalism abroad as well.[9]

In regard to church institutions, the conference encouraged total integration of colleges, children's homes, retirement homes, camps, and various other organizations among the Churches of Christ, as well as the implementation of dynamic minority appointment efforts for staff and boards of directors within these institutions. Regarding the Herald of Truth radio and television ministry specifically, the conference attendees voted to encourage more direct on-air statements addressing the sinfulness of racial discrimination and the inclusion of more African American speakers for its programs. The conference also urged Christian publishing companies to solicit more minority contributions to its publications and to publish more material concerning ongoing racial injustice. Members endorsed equal opportunity hiring practices among Christian-owned businesses and the establishment of training programs to enhance minority opportunities within these companies. They also argued for equal opportunities in housing, jobs, and education within American society in general. Combining church issues with social ones, the conference took a holistic approach to the problem of race relations by encouraging the exercise of political, social, economic, and religious pressure to support equal rights.[10] These proposals corresponded to what would become Mission's call to see social justice as an essential element of the gospel message. In a presentation made at the Detroit Race Relations Workshop later that year and published in *Mission*, Joseph F. Jones, Academic Vice President of Michigan Christian (now Rochester) College, summarized this understanding of the gospel. Jesus' life and teaching revealed that "the essence of religion [is] a love of God which manifests itself in undiscriminating concern and ministry for others."[11] Jones argued for a mutual responsibility of both black and white to identify and then remove walls that had brought discrimination and division: "It is our joint task to herald anew with bravery of heart, humility and love that reality which God produced but which sinful men have distorted, that 'there is neither black nor white in Christ.'"[12]

Predictably, this theology of reconciliation was met with charges that progressives were preaching a heretical "social gospel." Continuing to offer resistance, conservative Church of Christ leaders did not consider racial ethics to rest within the purview of restoration theology. To many church leaders, "faithful gospel preaching" was not compatible with the raw edges of life and ministry in the inner city. Church of Christ minister Glenn Wallace sounded the alarm: "They are set to RESTRUCTURE the church. They want our pulpits to ring with the social gospel theme. They want the 'urban ministry' to become the cry of our day. They are tired of the story of the 'old rugged cross.'"[13]

Encouraging self-evaluation among the Churches of Christ was tantamount to rejecting the very essence of the gospel itself. Thus, most southern church members continued to view racial integration as controversial and divisive. Perhaps James Bales best demonstrated this attitude in *The Martin Luther King Story* published in 1967. Bales charged King with being "an apostle of anarchy, apostasy, and appeasement . . . whose words and actions . . . would destroy America."[14] To sustain such an extreme position, Church of Christ leaders attempted to downplay the extent of racism in American society at large, to demonize civil rights advocates, and if forced to acknowledge (though faintly) the existence of racism, to feign impotence in finding a solution. W.B. Boyett, for instance, claimed, "Jesus Christ came into the world at a time when there was racial discrimination to an extent that has not been exceeded at any other period in history." For Boyett, because "Christ and the inspired apostles" did not organize marches, protests, and the like against racial discrimination, then his contemporary church leaders should not participate in such "unscriptural demonstrations" either.[15]

Weightier Matters

In an attempt to communicate the need for a new paradigm, Burch wrote an article entitled "Neglecting the Weightier Matters" published in the June 1968 issue of Firm Foundation. Anticipating Mission's challenge to the status quo, Burch concentrated on racial justice issues that would eventually become a hub for the journal's philosophical challenge to the old model. Burch chastised *Firm Foundation*'s constituency, observing that while the Churches of Christ had been quite willing to publicly oppose certain moral, social, and cultural sins—including evolutionary theory, alcohol sales, and gambling— they had been unwilling to exert their influence positively regarding racial injustice, a problem that Burch considered to be "the most flaming moral issue" within the entirety of Christian history. Incredibly, the Churches of Christ had been eager to "pull all [their] levers of influence, both public and private" to achieve the desired moral result in certain cases, but had refused to do so in the area of race relations. To Burch, this inconsistency was akin to the hypocrisy Jesus detected in the scribes and Pharisees—neglecting "the weightier matters of the law, justice and mercy and faith." In contrast to Burch's strategy, most church leaders believed that ending racial injustice, if such existed at all, was to be achieved gradually through the practice of preaching. While ending certain disfavored sins required immediate social action, racism's cure would take place in the heart, rather than in houses of worship or the halls of government. In response to this inaction, Burch closed the article with a question that cut to the heart of restoration theology— "Can the church continue knowingly to accommodate herself to prevailing racial prejudice and still be the church of Jesus Christ?"[16]

A strong reaction from *Firm Foundation*'s contributors resulted. Responding to Burch's essay, B. B. Harding expressed "wrath [and] disgust," accusing Burch of "sitting in the seat of the scoffer." To accept Burch's challenge would be to attempt to correct inequality in an unscriptural fashion. Instead, Harding recommended prayer, good deeds, and a Christ-like example in an atmosphere of law and order. He argued, "Each man is not to determine what is just or unjust, but obey the laws for the good of all; we want democracy—not anarchy." He accused Burch of attempting "to make [the church] a social, benevolent, or political club" and of being disrespectful "to God's family (and Christ's wife)."[17] Echoing Harding's defense of "law and order," *Firm Foundation* writer Ron Goodman criticized civil rights leaders like King of "rabble-rousing" by causing "rioting, burning, looting, and even death." Although slavery was actually a self-sustaining enterprise in the South by the mid-19th century, reflecting on the Civil War Era, Goodman lamented that "the nation by and large couldn't wait for the leavening influence of God-given principles to overcome slavery." Rather, people cried "unbiblical, unchristian, inhuman," resulting in "fighting and killing and the breeding of the worst kind of hate, though all of it was done in the name of freedom and racial injustice." It was the Civil War itself, according to Goodman, that caused such extreme animosity between the races.[18]

Contemporary appeals for racial justice would cause the same kind of hostility with deeper societal consequences. Preaching the gospel, living by it, and urging others to do the same was, for Goodman, the "only answer for a nation so nauseated that it has almost reached the point of regurgitation, and a world that has forgotten the meaning of peace and brotherly love."[19] Interestingly, Firm Foundation contributor Leon Barnes argued that it was actually impossible for the Churches of Christ to take a position on race relations without an established hierarchical structure. He observed that while "God is no respector [sic] of persons," this had no tangible influence on discrimination from a human perspective. In Barnes' judgment, Burch "ha[d] completely lost sight of the mission of the church." Finding only three authorized activities for the church—evangelization, edification, and benevolence—Barnes wondered, "under which of these, righting social wrongs, would fit."[20]

Mission Statements

It is within this polarizing atmosphere that Mission began publication in 1967 and immediately began challenging the Churches of Christ in regard to issues of discipleship, sacrifice, and "white flight." For instance, in the August 1967 issue of *Mission*, Locke equated the lack of ministry of the Churches of Christ within the inner cities to a lost emphasis on discipleship and a focus rather on mere "church membership."[21]

To begin its second year of publication in July 1968, *Mission* dedicated an issue to unsolicited articles received during the journal's first year. John McRay's article, "Race or Grace," provides a snapshot of the state of race relations within the fellowship as the 1960s drew to a close. McRay argued that the Churches of Christ needed self-evaluation regarding the issue of race more than any other institution or constituency. He charged church members with failing to live up to their restoration ideals. To McRay, identifying oneself with the New Testament church, while maintaining attitudes of white supremacy, deserved serious reflection. Church of Christ institutions, such as colleges, children's homes, and retirement communities in particular, deserved attention for their Jim Crow practices. He argued that segregationist policies within these institutions were aimed solely at expanding black marginalization. He complained, "It is a cause for shame among us that until recently our leading educational institutions affiliated with the church would admit people of every race but one." In comparing the treatment of blacks in the United States with that of Apartheid South Africa, McRay charged the Churches of Christ with focusing on less significant matters. Racial equality and social justice deserved the same attention as issues relating to foreign missions, church cooperation, and the like. Remarkably, McRay, a white minister and professor from Nashville, still viewed the issue through the lens of what had become the traditional Church of Christ theological approach. He emphasized the unchristian nature of violent protests and identified biblical reflection as the appropriate course of action. In so doing, McRay was relying on the time-honored proposition that in order to stop mistreatment based on race, one must first change the human heart. He specifically rejected the concepts of mass demonstrations and sit-ins as appropriate means for Christians to influence society. To participate in these activities was to admit failure on the part of the church and its mission: "If and when a church embarks upon campaigns that call for legal coercion, economic pressures in order to compel men to do their duty, then it has already failed in its primary goal."[22]

Despite lingering uneasiness among some contributors, in no other area was the distinction between Mission's approach and the so-called orthodox Church of Christ position more clearly seen than in the reaction to race riots like those that occurred in South Central Los Angeles in August 1965, as well as in Detroit and Newark in 1967. Representing the conservative majority, minister Robert R. Taylor, Jr., writing in Firm Foundation, criticized the *President's Commission on Civil Disorders* (1967) for not acknowledging "America's loss of God and his gospel." Expressing his frustration, Taylor objected:

> Proposed solutions centered around a greater measure of materialism offered to the disgruntled of our country. A better roof

over their heads, a job with higher pay to go to each day, more
food for their stomachs, better clothing and more "things" form
the projected panacea for the problems presently existing.[23]

In Mission, Jennings Davis, the Dean of Students at Pepperdine College
(now University), reflected on racial violence by considering the *President's
Commission* as well. However, unlike Taylor, Davis observed that it was
in fact white racism that had produced black alienation, rather than a
supposed widening rejection of the gospel. Quoting the commission's findings, Davis was critical of the development of "two societies, one black,
one white—separate and unequal." Davis agreed with the commission that
white terrorism was a significant contributing factor to such urban violent
responses: "Terrorism and violence perpetuated against blacks is the real
and sociologically significant kind of racial violence in our society." To
Davis, it was indeed a matter of law and order, but not in the sense assumed
by Taylor and his associates. Ironically, it was the rejection by state and local
officials of federal enforcement of civil rights regulations that had caused
such frustrated violence. Directly challenging the hypocrisy of the law and
order approach of the Churches of Christ, Davis declared:

> Between loud and pious rhetoric Sunday to Sunday, Negroes
> have been told that to be good Christians they must be obedi-
> ent servants. Told that "law and order" and "due process" are
> the keys to freedom. Negroes have watched racist governors,
> bigoted real estate dealers, prejudiced land lords [sic] and fright-
> ened personnel managers defy the laws, make shambles of order
> and forget due process in order that the god of white supremacy
> and a cherished "way of life" go undisturbed.[24]

In contrast, instead of acknowledging the culpability of white racism, T.J.
Finley, writing in *Firm* Foundation, saw a communist conspiracy. Claiming
"the war against Communism ... [was] being lost at home," Finley observed,
"leaders of mobs and movements may deny any Communist influence or
affiliation but their actions betray them." For Finley, to "act and talk like
Communists" assisted communist purposes. Quoting the Apostle Paul

("If a man does not work, neither let him eat."), he blamed the federal government for rewarding "laziness" and "the practice of illegitimacy." Thus, participants in civil disobedience were "endangering the security of the very country under whose protection they are allowed to act." Not surprisingly, he recommended a gradual process to help the aggrieved, complaining that "[t]he progress which could have come through time, effort, training, education, change of attitude, has been hindered while street marches and burnouts have become the order of the day."[25]

Writing in *Mission* two years later, Roosevelt C. Wells saw little value in such methodical progress. For Wells, a Church of Christ minister in Harlem, New York, nothing short of revolution would do: "A man cannot be honest, humanitarian, a sensitive Christian or American, have the experiences, exposures and knowledge I have about the plight of black people and their horrors in the inner city and not be a revolutionary." According to Wells, the white church had traded biblical values for an "Americanized" culture of white privilege and black exploitation. The only sufficient response to this prevailing notion of white supremacy was a full acceptance of black culture in America and in the American church. Such reception was required because, "The invisible black man is now very visible, and the silent black man is very verbal."[26] Consistent with Church of Christ theology, however, even the language of revolution needed spiritualization. As he explained:

> I seek not the blood of the oppressor, but a ban of his oppression.
> I seek not retribution for the racist, but repentence [sic] and
> retirement. I seek not the death of segregationists, but the death
> of segregation and scriptural sanctification for the segregating
> sinner. I seek not the destruction of our country, but the recon-
> struction of it.[27]

To Wells, the solution to the problem of racism was two-fold. First, within American culture at large, black separation was likely required. Because integration in terms of economics, housing, and education had been rejected by the majority, "Separatism [was] the black man's only answer." While segregation was based on the myth of white superiority, black separation was "a philosophy of equality and a strategy for survival," wherein African Americans could attain their full potentials.[28] Second, the American church had to create a reality that matched its rhetoric. Wells envisioned not just a body that theoretically claimed the characteristics of love, equality, and interdependence as its own, but one that practiced a "Christ-centered Christian unity," as "one in the church, one through the church, one because of the church." He concluded, "This is God's salvation. *Let us make it ours.*"[29]

Conclusion: In Black and White

The debate between those who advocated active removal of racial barriers within the Churches of Christ and those who argued for passive acceptance of existing conditions would continue in the pages of *Mission* and its conservative counterparts in the years that followed. Ron Durham (1931–2008), Church of Christ journalist, minister, and educator saw this debate metaphorically, as a mutual groping for a better day—

> Black,
> He looked for a black soul.
> Not for a part but the whole.
> Not as a gift or a grant,
> He looked for a root, not a plant.

> White,
> My own soul I possessed,
> Secure and at ease, at rest.
> Until his black agony
> Tore my white soul from me.

> Black and white,
> Both soulless, we two,
> Guilt-groping are looking for new
> Ways, and clearer weather.
> Now dare we grope together?[30]

Discussion Questions

1. In her monograph, *The History of White People* (Norton, 2010), historian Nell Irvin Painter argues that "race is an idea, not a fact." How does understanding race as sociological rather than biological help frame the discussion of race relations in the Churches of Christ?

2. Do you feel the gap between black and white in the Churches of Christ has widened or narrowed over the last thirty years? Why do you feel this way? What if we broadened the discussion to include Hispanics and Asians?

3. Would the Churches of Christ benefit from a conference on racial harmony today? How do you think such a meeting would be received?

4. Do Churches of Christ today tend to value opposition to certain moral or cultural sins while ignoring others? Can you give an example or two?

5. Compare and contrast how church leaders have responded to Black Lives Matter in recent years with how their predecessors reacted to racial protests in the 1960s. What similarities have you noticed? Differences?

Notes:

[1] Stanley Paregien, "Prejudiced—Who Me?," *Mission* 3,8 (February 1970): 241.

[2] Reuel Lemmons to John Allen Chalk, accessed March 9, 2016, http://webfiles.acu .edu/departments/Library/HR/restmov_nov11/www.mun.ca/rels/restmov/texts/race /haymes1.html/.

[3] Don Haymes, "Introduction to the Text," accessed March 9, 2016, http://webfiles.acu. edu/departments/Library/HR/restmov_nov11/www.mun.ca/rels/restmov/texts/race /haymes1.html/.

[4] Richard T. Hughes, *Reviving the Ancient Faith: The Story of Churches of Christ in America* (Abilene: Abilene Christian University Press, 1996), 270.

[5] Lynn McMillon, "A Conversation with Fred Gray," *Christian Chronicle* (February 17, 2008).

[6] Reuel Lemmons, "The Racial Problem," *Firm Foundation* 85,28 (July 9, 1968): 434.

[7] David Jones, Jr., "Growing Our Separate Ways," *Gospel Advocate* 132,1 (January 1990): 21.

[8] "The Atlanta Conference," *Mission* 2,3 (September 1968): 67.

[9] "Atlanta Race Relations Conference Lists Recommendations for Improvement," *Christian Chronicle* (July 12, 1968).

[10] Ibid.

[11] Joseph F. Jones, "In Christ: Neither Black nor White," *Mission* 3,1 (July 1969): 9–10.

[12] Ibid., 14.

[13] Glenn L. Wallace, "The Atlanta Conference," *First Century Christian* 2,4 (October 1968): 3.

[14] James D. Bales, *The Martin Luther King Story: A Study in Apostasy, Agitation, and Anarchy* (Tulsa: Christian Crusade, 1967), 8.

[15] W.B. Boyett, "Racial Discrimination," *Firm Foundation* 85, 28 (July 9, 1968): 435.

[16] Walter Burch, "Neglecting the Weightier Matters," *Firm Foundation* 85, 24 (June 11, 1968): 372.

[17] B. B. Harding, "Neglecting the Weightier Matters," *Firm Foundation* 85, 24 (June 11, 1968): 436.

[18] Ron Goodman, "Afterthoughts on 'Neglecting the Weightier Matters,'" *Firm Foundation* 85, 24 (June 11, 1968): 437.

[19] Ibid.

[20] Leon Barnes, "Should the 'Church of Christ' Take a Stand on Racial Discrimination?," *Firm Foundation* 85, 28 (July 9, 1968): 438.

[21] Hubert G. Locke, "Discipleship in the Inner City," *Mission* 1, 2 (August 1967): 52.

[22] John McRay, "Race or Grace," *Mission* 2, 1 (July 1968): 3–6.

[23] Robert R. Taylor, "The Omission of Jehovah," *Firm Foundation* 85, 24 (June 11, 1968): 439.

[24] Jennings Davis, "Racial Violence," *Mission* 2, 7 (January 1968): 218–220.

[25] T.J. Finley, "Turnpike to Tyranny," *Firm Foundation* 85, 22 (May 28, 1968): 340.

[26] Roosevelt C. Wells, "The Case for the Black Revolution," *Mission* 4, 1 (July 1970): 8–9.

[27] Ibid., 10.

[28] Ibid., 11.

[29] Ibid., 14.

[30] Ron Durham, "In Black and White," *Mission* 4, 2 (August 1970): 10.

The Gospel Is for All?

The Problem of Universality in J. M. McCaleb's Views on Missions and Race

by Yukikazu Obata

FOR THE PAST SEVERAL DECADES RACE HAS BEEN AN IMPORTANT issue in the historiography of Churches of Christ in the United States, especially regarding the black-white relationships. As the global development of the Stone-Campbell Movement is being considered today,[1] it seems opportune to look at race issues even beyond this domestic context.[2] In this chapter, I will examine the views on missions and race held by J. M. McCaleb (1861–1953), a pioneer missionary to Japan (1892–1941) and one who has been described as the father of overseas missions among the Churches of Christ.[3] As noted briefly by recent historians, McCaleb also engaged in discussions pertaining to race issues.[4]

In what follows, I will discuss McCaleb's understanding of missions, as well as his views on African Americans and Japanese people. In the end, I will attempt to demonstrate that undergirding McCaleb's views on missions and race is the paradoxical nature of universality, which might be behind today's racism as well.

McCaleb's Missionary Conviction: "The Gospel Is for All"

Central to McCaleb's missionary conviction was his belief in the universality of sin and the need for the gospel. Such conviction is clearly expressed in a hymn that he wrote in 1921, "The Gospel Is for All."

> 1. Of one the Lord has made the race,
> Thro' one has come the fall;
> Where sin has gone must go His grace,
> The Gospel is for all.
>
> 2. Say not the heathen are at home,
> Beyond we have no call,
> For why should we be blest alone?
> The Gospel is for all.[5]

In addition to the phrase "the gospel is for all," by which he meant the universal availability of the gospel, a key to understanding McCaleb's views on missions is his use of the word, "heathen." For McCaleb, heathenness is a universalistic notion that could be found either at home (in the United States) or abroad.[6] Through this understanding, McCaleb made a sweeping conclusion about the universal nature of humanity, a belief commonly expressed among the heirs of the European Enlightenment. In McCaleb's own words, "[that] Jesus died for all shows that all are of one nature and one blood."[7] Adopting doctrinal convictions connected with the modern notion of universality, McCaleb voluntarily engaged in innovative and sacrificial overseas missions that were mostly unpopular among the churches with which he associated.

McCaleb on African Americans

McCaleb's high regard for universality is also reflected in his views of African Americans, which he began to express following an experience he had during his first furlough. In 1899, he preached to African Americans near Lexington, Kentucky. He was excited about this opportunity but was saddened to hear that no Caucasian members of the Churches of Christ there had ever preached to African Americans.[8] McCaleb clearly recognized that "race prejudice . . . [stood] as a great barrier"[9] for the spread of the gospel. In this context, McCaleb, with his conviction of the "gospel is for all," resolved to preach to African Americans.[10]

After this experience, McCaleb wrote some accusatory articles in church papers to point out Caucasian Christians' prejudices. For example, he criticized wrong assumptions about African Americans' capability by citing one of Booker T. Washington's speeches that described successful African American endeavors. He also argued for the need to reach out to African Americans who needed salvation, "just the same as you and I."[11] McCaleb upheld universality when he wrote, "God has made of one all the nations to dwell upon the face of the earth. The fact that Jesus died for all shows that all are of one nature and one blood."[12]

As McCaleb continued to write about race issues, however, his own limitations became apparent. In 1907, McCaleb suggested that preacher-training schools, such as his alma mater College of the Bible, should admit African American students. His proposal was modest: "a few select" African American students should be admitted "into one corner to themselves" of the school.[13] McCaleb was immediately criticized for this limitation, and four months later, an African American preacher in Ohio took up what McCaleb had written stating, "[McCaleb's plan] is better than shutting the black boy out of school, but Bro. McCaleb should remember that the digressive brethren are doing better than he thinks already for the black boy."[14] When he replied to this criticism, McCaleb clarified his point of view on African Americans. Though he repeated his suggestion of admitting African American students to preacher-training schools, McCaleb added:

> There is a vast difference between them and us . . . . This differ-
> ence in race is the work of God and not of man. . . . [The African
> Americans] would remove the barriers that keep the white people
> from doing more for them, if that would cease their silly and
> unseemly efforts of trying to be the same as white people. Booker

Washington is doing a great work for his people in that he teaches them to be genuine Negroes and not try to be white folks.[15]

As such, historian Edward Robinson views McCaleb as a "racial conservative," even among his contemporary Caucasian members of the Churches of Christ. McCaleb's conservativism is attested further when he wrote, "it is folly to attempt a visionary plan without regard to conditions. In the North they tolerate a few blacks mixed miscellaneously in the classes of the whites, but this will not work in the South. We must deal with conditions as they are, and not as we think they ought to be."[16]

So, while McCaleb advocated the need to preach to African Americans, the conservative nature of his racial understanding surfaced when he discussed the inclusion of African Americans in the training of preachers. Why was his view on race so limited, even though he upheld the universalistic motto of the "gospel is for all" that seemed to support equality of race? McCaleb's views on race in the Japanese context will be helpful to solve this riddle.

McCaleb on Japanese People

In Japan, McCaleb practiced exactly what he had said should be done in the case of African Americans, namely evangelism and moral training. McCaleb also dealt with different aspects of racial issues in Japan as he lived in that country more than four decades.

As missiologist Ed Matthews has noted, during his long period of service in Japan, McCaleb did not fully immerse himself in the Japanese culture. He was not comfortable living in the Japanese-style houses or eating Japanese food.[17] His view on Japanese race is symbolically expressed in his opposition to racially mixed marriage, which is quintessential of racial prejudice. McCaleb wrote that US-Japanese marriages had to be discouraged because of cultural and religious differences, as well as of health reasons, saying that Japanese had "hereditary and dreadful diseases."[18] Of course, McCaleb did recognize some good in the Japanese society. For example, McCaleb once wrote he was very impressed with the cleanliness of Japanese trains, compared to ones he knew in the United States. But then, he used the description of such differences as a lesson for people back home, saying that the Anglo-Saxon, who was "so much superior," can still learn from the Japanese, who belonged to the yellow Mongolian."[19]

To be sure, seeing the Japanese culture and race as inferior was not unique to McCaleb, even among those who engaged in world missions. For example, A. B. Simpson (1843–1919), McCaleb's contemporary and a strong advocate of world missions as the founder of Christian and Missionary Alliance, described Japanese people as "frightfully immoral," evidenced by women's clothing and the custom of public baths.[20]

In fact, recognizing the inferiority of others was part of the motivation for missions. According to McCaleb, "that the Western nations have a civilization superior to the East is generally admitted,"[21] and he attributed Christianity as the very reason for the superiority. In a reply to a fellow US citizen who asked McCaleb why the western nations were advanced, McCaleb admitted that it may have something to do with "the superiority of Anglo-Saxon race," but he emphasized that the heart of the matter was the pagan religions of "the Oriental nations."[22] Thus, McCaleb engaged in evangelism and moral training of Japanese people so that they would acquire Christian faith, which would lead to the advancement of morality and civilization.

One might suppose that McCaleb's missionary conviction and his notion of universal humanity would have led him to reject racial prejudice. However, his understanding of the universality of the gospel did not challenge his underlying assumptions concerning his own racial superiority.

Universality and Cultural Imperialism

Significantly, McCaleb's education and initial missionary work in Japan took place during the period of what historians call high imperialism (1880–1920). The genius of high imperialism, especially in the case of the United States, was that it did not simply consist of military power. Stronger emphasis was placed upon certain universalistic *values* such as philanthropism and morality.[23] The underlying rationale hidden behind this "generous imperialism" was social Darwinism which suggested that stronger nations were meant to survive at the top of the totem pole. Those who were ethnically superior were equipped with civility, which inferior nations (often described as "the heathen" or "savages") had yet to possess.

For missionaries of this era, as missiologist David Bosch has noted, the exportation of such values was understood to be a Christian duty, a debt that Christians "owed those who still dwelt 'in darkness and the shadow of death.'"[24] In other words, there was a tendency to equate Western civilization with Christian civilization, and in that understanding the "burden" of Christian missions was to bring such advanced civilization to the uncivilized. When the particularity of Western culture is imposed upon others in the name of universality—Christian or otherwise—such imposition becomes cultural imperialism.[25]

Although labeling Western missionaries as cultural imperialists is too simplistic, McCaleb was certainly a product of his time, sharing the basic ethos of high imperialism. McCaleb was not hesitant to talk about the superiority of Western civilization and noted that the United States was "the most enlightened nation in the world."[26] He also wrote, as late as 1934, "that the Western nations have a civilization superior to the East is generally admitted."[27] Mission historian Shawn Daggett does not exaggerate when he wrote that McCaleb's "dream of educating and civilizing as a foundation for evangelism, carried an unstoppable inertia."[28]

Universality and Racism

The French philosopher Etienne Balibar has noted that the notion of universality does not simply bring forth cultural imperialism; more importantly, it constructs racism.[29] The mechanism of universality is paradoxical. On the one hand, universality expresses such ideals of equality and freedom that have the potential to eliminate racism. On the other hand, "universality is paradoxically present in racism itself."[30] As the philosopher Naoki Sakai explains, such racism emerges in the process of the construction of modern nation-states. Universalistic ideals, such as equality and liberty, play a significant role in the formation of a nation. In the end, however, the equality is granted only to those who were fixed by the state as proper nationals. Thus, such fixation also gives birth to the "others" (or "inferior races"), who may be inside or outside the state.[31] This understanding of the connection between universality and racism is important, as it indicates that racism is not an expression of some vulgar ethnocentrism or obsolete particularism modern people have (supposedly) learned to abandon.[32]

In fact, one could argue that McCaleb's high regard for universality had the potential of articulating racism. Upon visiting Africa during a world tour of 1929 McCaleb wrote, "I am inclined to think the African is better off under European rule than when left to himself."[33] Again, such a notion is not uncommon in this era when Africa was tragically designated as a "dark continent." What should be noted here are the ways in which universality was at work, perhaps unconsciously, in what McCaleb was writing, in both his discourse of civilizing mission and racialization of Africa. Following Balibar, McCaleb's potential racism can be explained as the consequence of having a fixed notion of what constitutes proper Christians.

Concluding Remarks

McCaleb's strong conviction on the universality of the gospel and of humanity, expressed in the phrase the "gospel is for all," and the flaw in his views on race were not necessarily contradictory. Rather, these apparently opposing views were both expressions of his paradoxical views on universality. The motto of "the gospel is for all" is certainly rooted in the Bible and was an impetus for McCaleb's long-lasting mission work, but the above discussion made clear that such a motto of universality was not sufficient by itself as a discourse to reject racism.

Finally, if McCaleb's ambiguity on race issues derives from his adoption of the modern ideal of universality, not some vulgar ethnocentrism or obsolete particularism, it means that the problem of racism is likely an on-going problem, even among today's better-educated Christians. Balibar reminds us that racism is quite a "modern" invention and could be present in any modern nation-state. The paradox of universality could continue to haunt us, especially if we ignore history. Thus, this historical inquiry reveals what was involved in the remarkable achievement of this "father of missions." When coupled with a proper appreciation for his contribution, McCaleb's life and commitment to sharing the good news can be a challenge for all of us who continue to deal with the issue of racism today.

Discussion Questions

1. Based on what you know about the social context of the South in early twentieth century, how would you evaluate the views McCaleb expressed on race issues?

2. If you are to become a missionary or supporter of missions, would you make use of McCaleb's motto, "the gospel is for all"? If yes, how? If no, why not?

3. Why can upholding universality in Christian missions be imperialistic?

4. Etienne Balibar suggests that universality does not simply bring forth cultural imperialism; instead, it constructs racism. How could the notion of universality lead to racism?

5. In your society or community, who are the "proper" members and who are not? Discuss how such distinction was (or is being) made.

Notes:

[1] Gary Holloway and Douglas A. Foster, *Renewing the World: A Concise Global History of the Stone-Campbell Movement* (Abilene Christian University Press, 2015).

[2] For example, W. E. B. Dubois considered race issues of Asia. Samuel Cassius was inspired by Japan missionary F. A. Wagner. Cassius and Japanese preacher Hirosuke Ishiguro encouraged Japan missionary Hettie Lee Ewing. E. W. McMillan served as president at both Southwestern Christian College and Ibaraki Christian College. See Bill V. Mullen and Cathryn Watson, eds., *W. E. B. Du Bois on Asia: Crossing the World Color Line* (Jackson: University Press of Mississippi, 2005); Edward J. Robinson, *To Save My Race from Abuse: The Life of Samuel Robert Cassius* (Tuscaloosa: University of Alabama Press, 2007), 24; S. H. Hall, "The Ishiguro Mission," *Gospel Advocate* (September 3, 1925): 842; Robert M. Randolph, "Growing Up Campbelite, 1940–2004: What We Said and What We Did," *Restoring The First-century Church in the Twenty-first Century: Essays on the Stone-Campbell Restoration Movement: In Honor of Don Haymes*, ed. Warren Lewis and Hans Rollmann (Eugene, OR: Wipf and Stock Publishers, 2005), 504–505.

[3] Alan Henderson, "A Historical Review of Missions and Missionary Training in the Churches of Christ," *Restoration Quarterly* 35,4 (1993): 204. For a helpful biographical sketch of and recent works on McCaleb, see: Jeremy P. Hegi, "McCaleb, John Moody (1861–1953): Pioneer Missionary for Churches of Christ," in *History of Missiology*, Boston University School of Theology, accessed November 20, 2015, http://www.bu.edu/missiology/missionary-biography/l-m/mccaleb-john-moody-1861-1953/.

[4] Robinson, *To Save My Race from Abuse*: 64–66; Edward J. Robinson, *Show Us How You Do It: Marshall Keeble and the Rise of Black Churches of Christ in the United States, 1914–1968* (Tuscaloosa: University of Alabama Press, 2008), 32; Matthew C. Cass, "Race Relations and New Testament Identity in Churches of Christ, 1900–1929" (master's thesis, Abilene Christian University, 2005).

[5] This hymn first appeared in *Great Songs of the Church, No. 1*, (1921) ed. E. L. Jorgenson. The complete lyrics of the song are available at: "The Gospel is For All," in *The Cyber Hymnal*, accessed November 20, 2015, http://www.hymntime.com/tch/htm/g/o/s/gosisfor.htm/.

[6] J. M. McCaleb, *Once Traveled Roads* (Nashville: Gospel Advocate Company, 1934), 436–438.

[7] J. M. McCaleb, "The Negro," *Gospel Advocate* (March 17, 1904): 166.

[8] J. M. McCaleb, "In Louisville," *Gospel Advocate* (October 12, 1899): 655.

[9] J. M. McCaleb, "Japan Letter: A Plea for the Colored Man," *Christian Leader and the Way* (January 1, 1907): 2.

[10] J. M. McCaleb, "The African at Our Door," *World Vision* (June, 1937): 4–5.

[11] J. M. McCaleb, "The Negro," *Gospel Advocate* (June 4, 1903): 358.

[12] McCaleb, "Negro (1904)," 166. Commenting on these views, historian Don Haymes wrote that McCaleb had "a truly 'global' consciousness long before it was fashionable—nay, before it was *possible!*" Don Haymes, "Introduction to the Text, 'The Negro' by John Moody McCaleb, Race and the Church of Christ," accessed August 22, 2015, http://webfiles.acu.edu/departments/Library/HR/restmov_nov11/www.mun.ca/rels/restmov/texts/race/haymes2.html.

[13] McCaleb, "Plea for the Colored Man," 2.

[14] M. F. Womack, "A Training School for Disciples of African Descent," *Christian Leader and the Way* (May 21, 1907): 2.

[15] J. M. McCaleb, "The Koishikawa Church," *Christian Leader and the Way* (February 9, 1909): 3.

[16] Ibid.

[17] Ed Mathews, "McCaleb, John Moody," in *The Encyclopedia of the Stone-Campbell Movement*, ed. Douglas A. Foster, et al. (Grand Rapids, MI: Wm. B. Eerdmans Publishing Co., 2004), 506. See also J. M. McCaleb, "Should Americans and Japanese Marry?," *Gospel Advocate* (October 24, 1906): 679.

[18] Gary Owen Turner, "Pioneer to Japan: a Biography of J. M. McCaleb" (master's thesis, Abilene Christian College, 1972), 206.

[19] J. M. McCaleb, "Missionary Notes," *Firm Foundation*, April 30, 1901, 4.

[20] Simpson, *Larger Outlooks on Missionary Lands* (New York, 1893), 541–543; quoted in William R. Hutchison, *Errand to the World: American Protestant Thought and Foreign Missions* (Chicago: University of Chicago Press, 1987), 116.1987

[21] McCaleb, *Once Traveled Roads*: 193–194.

[22] J. M. McCaleb, *On the Trail of the Missionaries* (Nashville: Gospel Advocate, 1930), 85.

[23] Amy Kaplan and Donald E. Pease, eds., *Cultures of United States Imperialism* (Durham, NC: Duke University Press, 1993).

[24] David J. Bosch, *Transforming Mission: Paradigm Shifts in Theology of Mission*, Twentieth Anniversary ed. (Maryknoll, NY: Orbis Books, 2011), 292.

[25] Scott W. Sunquist, *Understanding Christian Mission: Participation in Suffering and Glory* (Grand Rapids, Baker Academic, 2013), 99, 244.

[26] J. M. McCaleb, "Moving Pictures," *Firm Foundation* (January 24, 1939), 2.

[27] McCaleb, *Once Traveled Roads*: 193–194.

[28] Shawn Z. Daggett, "The Lord Will Provide: James A. Harding, J. M. McCaleb, William J. Bishop, and the Emergence of Faith Missions in the Churches of Christ, 1892–1913" (Th.D diss., School of Theology, Boston University, 2007), 232.

[29] Balibar, "Racism and Nationalism," 62.

[30] Balibar, "Preface," 9.

[31] Naoki Sakai, "Subject and Substratum: On Japanese Imperial Nationalism," *Cultural Studies* 14,3/4 (2000): 462–530.

[32] Balibar, "Racism and Nationalism," 49–50.

[33] McCaleb, *On the Trail of the Missionaries*: 160.

People of Faith at the Racial Barricades

Little Rock, Arkansas 1957

by John Mark Tucker

What occurred to me then and still strikes me now is how much of the painful past we have yet to confront, even when we love each other and think that we know one another. So much of what agonizes and divides us remains unacknowledged.

Why linger on the past, which we cannot change? We must move toward a brighter future and leave all that horror behind . . . . We must make a new world. But we can't make it out of whole cloth. We have to weave the future from the fabric of the past, from the patterns of aspiration and belonging—and broken dreams and anguished rejections—that have made us.

What the advocates of our dangerous and deepening social amnesia don't understand is how deeply the past holds the future in its grip—even, and perhaps especially, when it remains unacknowledged. We are runaway slaves from our own past, and only by turning to face the hounds can we find our freedom beyond them.[1]

—*Timothy B. Tyson*

When Central High School opened in 1927, the American Institute of Architects designated it "America's Most Beautiful High School." The *New York Times* described Central as the most expensive school ever built in the United States. Whatever the value of these claims, it was most improbable that a structure of such magnificence arose in a poverty-stricken southern state. The building is, indeed, imposing: six stories covering two city blocks, with 100 classrooms, a 2,000-seat auditorium, a gymnasium, a greenhouse, a reflecting pool, and eventual student capacity of 2,400. Anyone pursuing an education would be impressed by Central. People of color had been kept out for thirty years but that was destined to change.[2]

But the year 1927 was memorable for a sinister reason. A black man, accused of a crime, was hanged without a trial, shot, dragged into a black neighborhood, and set on fire, an event inevitably seared into the minds of black parents rearing their children in the 1950s. Unfortunately, our national character features "white riots": whites killing blacks without provocation, due process, or equality before the law. Our black holocaust, as some call it, dates from the earliest days of our republic.[3] But 1927 also offered a glimmer of hope for people of faith. The Pulaski Heights Christian Church was established at the corner of Spruce Street and Hillcrest Avenue, becoming a beacon for social justice. This church emerged as a vital partner in the civil rights movement of the 1950s, even as it had served the needs of Japanese-Americans in prison camps during the previous decade.

When civic leaders resolved to integrate Central, the remnants of three milestones each thirty years of age—a landmark building, a lynch mob, and a Christian church—would be woven into the fabric of 1957. A carefully scripted strategy for integration would signal a new era, leading the city and state out of isolation and poverty by building businesses and schools for a better life. Little Rock could become a leader, implementing the US Supreme Court's decision in *Brown vs. Board of Education of Topeka* (1954) supporting integration. In fact, former Arkansas governor, Sid McMath, stated that Little Rock should have been the "last place" for a crisis, "because we were making so much progress, and the people had been accepting [integration] in a proper frame of mind."[4] Virgil T. Blossom, ambitious Superintendent of Schools, planned to implement integration gradually, hoping for a peaceful process. He would build public support, offer a model for other cities, develop a following, and run for governor. To ensure success, he personally interviewed and selected the nine students he (and the principals and teachers from the separate black schools) believed could endure a tough regimen of constant harassment and academic rigor.[5]

The Little Rock School Board and Organized Resistance

But Blossom miscalculated. His prior success in Fayetteville and his roots in Missouri did not prepare him for the backlash overtaking Little Rock. He had no ties to blue collar whites, hard-working, church-going citizens who regarded segregation as sanctioned by God and integration as inspired by Communism. Governor Orval Faubus had promised these "little people," as he referred to them—waitresses, hairdressers, shop keepers, file clerks, farm workers, and truck drivers—that he would not support integration.[6] The elites, Blossom's natural constituents, were too genteel, too passive, and too comfortable to counteract segregationists' rapid response.

Working class people doubted civic leaders with good reason. The School District had constructed Hall High School in west Little Rock and Horace Mann High School on the east side, Hall for whites and Horace Mann for blacks. Thus, an all-white school in Pulaski Heights served people of wealth and, when parents complained about integration at Central, Blossom told them to move to the Heights, something few could afford. The Superintendent and members of the Board all lived in the Heights, allowing them a cushion of white supremacy and privilege. Still, Little Rock would integrate Central High, and present itself to the nation as a modern, progressive city.[7]

This obvious duplicity angered segregationists. When some of them lashed out, they threatened board members and other civic leaders. As the 1957 school year approached, reports of organized violence increased dramatically. Gun sales rose in Pulaski County, and caravans of agitators were rumored to be headed for Little Rock. Blossom and the Board feared for their lives, having received anonymous phone calls and bomb threats. They conducted their business in secret, hired state troopers to guard their homes, and sent their own children to school out of Little Rock or even out of state.[8]

Wayne Upton was well-connected, presiding over the Episcopal Churchman's Association of Arkansas, the Pulaski County Bar Association, and the Little Rock School Board. A confidante of Virgil Blossom, he was also my mother Edith's older brother. She and Wayne and their sister, Becky (Board), grew up in northwest Tennessee, west of Obion near Reelfoot Lake. Wayne Upton was smart, wry, funny, and philosophical about life but opinionated about people and politics. Obion was an oasis for the Huffstutter, Tucker, and Upton families, and I first heard about Orval Faubus, Virgil Blossom, and Daisy Bates at family reunions when Uncle Wayne was telling stories. I lacked interest and understanding at the time but would learn much later that Wayne had played a pivotal role in the saga of Little Rock.

Daisy Bates and the Little Rock Nine

Daisy Bates was President of the Arkansas NAACP, a thorn in the side of the Superintendent and the Board. She supported the Little Rock Nine (as they were soon known), having become their liaison with the Superintendent, attorneys, police, and the press, and she reassured and encouraged their families. The nine students, seeking opportunity at great risk, were Minnijean Brown (Trickey), Elizabeth Eckford, Ernest Green, Thelma Mothershed (Mothershed-Wair), Melba Patillo (Beals), Gloria Ray (Kalmark), Terrence Roberts, Jefferson Thomas (1942–2010), and Carlotta Walls (LaNier). Some regarded Daisy Bates and her husband, L. C., as over-bearing but they effectively surrounded the students with civil rights activists, shielding the kids from violence, and paid a heavy price, with broken windows, bomb threats, shootings, cross-burnings, and loss of the family business.

On September 4th 1957, Elizabeth Eckford prepared for her first day in a racially integrated school by reading these words, "Hear me when I call, O God of my righteousness: thou hast enlarged me when I was in distress; have mercy upon me, and hear my prayer . . . . Wait on the Lord: be of good courage, and he shall strengthen thine heart: wait, I say, on the Lord" (Psalms 4:1; 27:14 KJV). She rode a city bus a portion of the way, and walked alone to Central High School. When Eckstrom saw the Arkansas National Guard, she thought initially they would protect her, but Governor Faubus had instructed the Guard to turn black students away. With her entrance blocked, Eckstrom decided to go back home. As she headed for a nearby bus stop, Eckstrom was soon engulfed by a mob shouting, cursing, spitting, and threatening her life. Photographer Will Counts, representing the *Arkansas Gazette*, took Eckstrom's picture as she moved forward surrounded by enraged protesters.

The Counts photo, shown across the globe, became iconic in US history, earning a Pulitzer Prize and recognition by the Associated Press as among the 100 most important photographs of the twentieth century. The photograph, a stark image frozen in time, reveals Eckford on the right, stoic, wearing dark glasses, carrying a notebook; slightly left and behind Eckford is Hazel Bryan, face drawn in anger and apparently shouting a racial epithet.

According to Bryan, "her parents were 'very racially prejudiced,' as were all of the whites of their acquaintance. A member of the Church of Christ, which was among the most rigid practitioners of Christian fundamentalism, Bryan never heard directly from the pulpit that the races should be kept separate. But in thinking back to those days, Bryan recalls, "You always got the idea you weren't supposed to marry, intermarry.'"[9]

Eckford finally reached a bus stop, sat down, and began to wait. Thankfully, the Lord sent a *New York Times* reporter and a civil rights activist to protect her from the racist crowd following her. Eckford's first day at Central was supposed to be much different. Daisy Bates had planned to lead the students as a group, surrounded by supporters, and enter a side door. Overcome with last minute details, Bates forgot to tell Eckford that they would walk together. The Eckfords, while a middle class family, had no telephone.

Inside the Building

Superintendent Blossom established ground rules for the Little Rock Nine. Carlotta Walls remembered the meeting Blossom called with the students and their parents.

> We might hear some name calling, he said, but we were not
> to retaliate in any way. For our own safety . . . we would have
> to leave the school grounds as soon as our classes ended. That
> meant we would not be allowed to participate in any extracur-
> ricular activities—no varsity sports, clubs, chorus, band or even
> the Student Government Association. We also could not attend
> any after-school parties or sporting events.[10]

Inside the building, an angry group of white students targeted the black students for abuse, hoping to drive them out. Student agitators spewed curses and racial epithets, threw pencils and spitballs, and they covered doors, windows, and walls with racist graffiti. White students shoved the black students, kicked them, and spit on them. White agitators threw broken glass into shower stalls and scalded the black students with hot water. Black students would enter a bathroom stall, and white students would follow them into the restroom, strike a match, light a paper towel, and throw it over the top of the stall. Eckford was pushed down a flight of stairs. Jefferson Thomas was knocked unconscious. During 1957–58, Central endured forty-three bomb threats, each of which required police to clear 2,000 lockers. On October 3rd 1957, a white students hung a black body in effigy. A revisionist narrative aims to soften the edges, to minimize the severity of the harassment, to whitewash the abuse but, thankfully, written accounts by several of the Nine have preserved their eyewitness account. These were not high school hijinks; they were acts of terror, calculated, vicious, hate-filled, and sustained.[11]

During the 1957–58 school year, a white student attacked Melba Patillo with acid. A soldier, responding quickly, saved her eyesight. Someone bombed the home of Carlotta Walls. No one was ever charged with that crime. Some parents of the Nine, as well as relatives and friends, lost their jobs. Years later, Eckford recalled that only five white students at Central had been kind to her. When Minnijean Brown retaliated and was expelled from school, white students displayed signs reading, "one down, eight to go." School officials minimized the terror, trying to prove the success of their integration plan, and authorities chose not to prosecute. One reporter construed broadly but accurately that unruly mobs had first gathered in the street, then simply moved inside the building.[12] In her memoir, Carlotta Walls cited the one place at Central where she was safe.

> It was really just a large classroom, filled with desks and chairs, on the main level of the school. But for twenty minutes each morning, before classes began, the classroom became a place of meditation and prayer . . . . There was no interaction between the black and white students, but I knew that at least we had come there for a common purpose: to pray . . . . The program generally included a Bible reading, prayer, and hymns—my favorite part of the service, especially the old standard "Amazing Grace". . . . This became my haven, the place where I found the spiritual fuel I needed to get through each day. I felt the presence of God there. In those moments, it never occurred to me to ask God, "Why so much pain?" When I thought about Jesus Christ and the profound suffering he endured, that made my own challenges seem small. I told myself that I could surely go on.[13]

Lives after High School

Hazel Bryan left Central and attended Fuller High School, a county school. She upset her parents by marrying a Catholic, Antoine Massery, but she converted him to her faith. They attended the Arch Street Church of Christ where Massery became a deacon and Bryan a teacher. Relative stability yielded the potential for self-reflection. Bryan grew deeply distressed that the photograph of her yelling obscenities at Eckford was seen around the world. She realized that she would one day have to explain it to her children. In 1963, Bryan reached out to Eckford to ask for forgiveness. Bryan recalls,

> I just told her who I was—I was the girl in that picture that was
> yelling at her, that I was sorry, that it was a terrible thing to do
> and that I didn't want my children to grow up to be like that,
> and I was crying.[14]

Eckford accepted her apology because Bryan seemed sincere and so desperately desired forgiveness. Furthermore, Eckford was urged to to accept Bryan's apology by her father and grandfather.[15]

Bryan struggled at the Arch Street congregation. She describes the congregation as regimented and racially intolerant. Bryan was eventually disfellowshipped from the congregation, perhaps due to her flirtation with New Age religion, her work as a belly dancer, or her more enlightened attitude toward black people.

Eckford and her family attended the Union African Methodist Episcopal Church, a denomination that has a long history of resistance to social injustices. Despite enduring some of the most egregious abuse from white students, Eckford wanted to stay at Central High. She shielded her parents from awareness of the most flagrant abuse. Her family, as did the families of the other Nine, suffered retaliation. Eckford's mother was fired from the Arkansas School for the Deaf and Blind Negro, where she taught laundry skills. Eckford's grandfather, highly respected by both blacks and whites, who owned a small grocery store, had a brick thrown through the front window of his store.[16] Eckford did not graduate from Central High School because all Little Rock schools were closed the following year.

However, she completed her high school degree in Missouri. She went on to earn a History degree from Central State University in Ohio. Following college and five years of military service, Eckford returned to Little Rock. She said, "I came back because I felt I was chased away and because I thought it was cowardly, and I wanted to prove I could live in this situation. . . . I don't intend to be driven out." She added, "No matter what you have in terms of economic security... in terms of self-confidence, if you are black you are vulnerable—vulnerable to losing everything you have."[17]

Due to her experience at Central High School, Eckford has battled severe depression and post-traumatic stress disorder.[18] Life for Eckford has been difficult. She raised her two sons on a meager disability income, the constants being her two-bedroom home and her amazing flower garden. Always strong in her relationship with God, Eckford believed that certain matters must be faced with prayer. She tended to ask the Creator for strength and peace rather than for material things. In 1992, her health improved, she began a career as a probation officer, moving beyond the pit of despair.[19]

Orval Faubus served as governor of the state of Arkansas from 1955 to 1964. He is best known for his stance against the federal order to desegregate the state's public schools. He called the Arkansas National Guard to Central High School to "maintain order." Faubus goes on to say that the Guard "will not act as segregationists or integrationists".[20] He vowed to protect the southern way of life for the "little people," complaining bitterly about the largely integrationist Little Rock School Board. As the 1958 fall semester approached, the citizens of Little Rock voted to close the high schools rather than integrate them. Opposed by the Governor and the city, all but one member of the School Board resigned in protest and Superintendent Blossom was fired. During the 1958–59 academic year, schools were closed. Although classrooms were empty, approximately 200 teachers and administrators, who were still under contract, continued to report to work. There were approximately forty-four teachers fired because of their pro-integration stance.[21] The only regular activity of the public high schools that year was Central High School football.[22]

Little Rock School Board president Wayne Upton (1957–58) favored integration, reasoning that it was the law of the land and the right thing to do. He had grown up in the Churches of Christ. His father, my grandfather Colpy Upton, had been a pillar of the community, who managed a general store, donated groceries and dry goods to help his neighbors through the

Great Depression, and paid for construction of a new building for the Oak Ridge Church of Christ.

An impulse toward public service, not surprisingly, animated Wayne Upton. He regarded the task of the Christian as helping those in need. Upton knew "deep down" that segregation was not defensible, that it was unreasonable to deny blacks equal opportunity, and that integration was right on the basis of "sound Christian principles."[23] Upton contributed to a news column, "What My Religion Means to Me," promoting the love of God and the love of neighbor as foundational to prudent personal behavior and essential for the common good. These two commandments, he added, "as a day to day mode of living can have no other result than to strengthen each of us individually and to weld us into a stronger nation."[24] Whatever we might claim for Upton in the way of right morality, the School Board under Upton's leadership has drawn serious historical rebuke. Karen Anderson, for instance, described the Board as uncertain of its principles, lacking political convictions and courage, and bound by its own sense of victimization. Sondra Gordy described the Board as interested only in minimal, token integration, and she accused its members of moral failure by not standing up for desegregation, arguing, in concert with historian John Kirk, that the Board's tepid approach was counterproductive, serving perhaps inadvertently to feed the forces of massive resistance.[25]

The Next Year: Advantage of White Privlege

Moral ambivalence, even in the face of threatened violence, must be considered moral failure in the context of suffering endured by black people. The insidious nature of white supremacy nurtured among whites is an instinctive response, if not a cognitive decision, to not confront horror directly but—in equally ghastly fashion—to simply look away from it, or to be conditioned to actually not see what is plainly in sight. A statement by Gayle Singleton (Gardner), a white woman who was a student at an area school, illustrates this complexity. During the 1958–59 academic year, when the Little Rock high schools were closed, nearly 3,700 students and their parents were forced to fend for themselves. Students moved away from home to room and board with relatives or friends. Others endured lengthy commutes. A few groups of students met in community centers, taking correspondence courses together. Governor Faubus provided fifteen white teachers who taught courses on television for students out of school. A number of students attended segregated private academies. Many students dropped out, went to work or joined the military, and never obtained a high school diploma. Gardner attended the all-white Hall High School in 1957–58 and Baptist High, a segregated private academy, the following year. Her family favored segregation. Gardner mellowed over the years, now realizing that segregation was wrong. Maybe she was influenced by her brother, a Methodist minister, or by her husband who had witnessed first-hand the rioting at Central High. Gardner was questioned years later about the time the Little Rock schools were closed. When asked if she knew that blacks had been locked out of their own school, Horace Mann High, Gardner replied, "I am embarrassed—I am embarrassed [to learn that]. I did not realize that."[26]

Likewise benefitting from white privilege, integration advocate Colbert S. Cartwright displayed no ambivalence. A graduate of Yale and the son of a minister, Cartwright pastored the Pulaski Heights Christian Church. The first Sunday following the Supreme Court's *Brown vs Board of Education* decision, Cartwright preached a sermon urging compliance. Excerpts from this sermon was printed in the *Arkansas Gazette* . In 1956, he chaired the Arkansas Council on Human Relations which was instrumental in merging separate white and black ministerial groups into the Little Rock Ministerial Association. Gardner collaborated with Quakers and Methodists on a series of interracial conferences, and he joined Daisy Bates, Will D. Campbell, and other activists in escorting the Little Rock Nine into Central High. His pro-integration stance drew intense criticism. In the fall of 1957, thirty-one of his 310 members departed his congregation in protest.[27]

The Face of Reconciliation:
Revisiting Relationships in the Photograph

In 1997, there was an event, hosted by President Bill Clinton and Arkansas Governor Mike Huckabee, commemorating forty years since the desegregation of Central High School. Will Counts, who took the original photograph, coordinated an introduction between Hazel Bryan Massery and Elizabeth Eckford. This marked the first time that two women talked face-to-face. Eckford was better read, better educated, and more articulate. Bryan was more creative, more practical, and more sociable. Both are more introspective than those around them. They had few confidantes, seldom fitting easily with family or community. Bryan was estranged from her high school classmates. She, more publicly than anyone, had stepped forward to confess her sins. She would take the heat forever without a supportive friend from childhood. Eckford, on the other hand, unlike the other eight students, never gloried in her achievement. She was a casualty, deeply-scarred, suspicious of publicity and organized events and, sometimes, of her new friend, Hazel Bryan Massery. Their relationship has had ups and downs, but their initial togetherness was inspirational.[28] It had begun with much promise, and they had reached out to one another, crossing the barricades of suspicion and hate. Activist Will Campbell described the dream, "the beauty of the God-made deep black skin of the one seems to enhance the same made and equally beautiful ice-white skin of the other;" their friendship was "the stuff of scripture . . . . [it gave us all] a glimpse of the Promised Land."[29]

Eckford and Bryan forged a friendship where they traveled together speaking to various groups. They visited flower shows and bought fabrics together. They even wrote a book together.[30] There were many who were skeptical of Bryan's quest for racial reconciliation. While eager to be seen in solidarity with Eckford in front of cameras, Bryan often lamented that Eckford received more attention than she did. Blacks and whites often observed the lack of sincerity in Bryan's efforts, but it took a little longer for Eckford to see it. Eckford began seeing inconsistencies in Bryan's recounting of her role in the treatment of the Little Rock Nine. Eckford suggested that Bryan was "seeking forgiveness on the cheap, without any pain or introspection." Eckford recounts, "She wanted me to be cured and be over it and for this not to go on anymore. She wanted me to be less uncomfortable so that she wouldn't feel responsible."[31]

The 1997 photograph of the two women in front of Central High School was seen as a manifestation of Eckford's forgiveness of Bryan. It also suggested that the two women were on a road of reconciliation. However, that path of reconciliation was relatively short lived. By the early 2000s, the women were no longer speaking to each other.[32] At the second printing of the poster, a quote from Eckford was added: "True reconciliation can only occur when we honestly acknowledge our painful, but shared, past."[33]

Bryan later complained that she was not consulted on the second print-ing of the poster. She has reportedly stated that she would like to have a quote of her own added to the poster: "True reconciliation can occur only when we honestly let go of resentment and hatred, and move forward."[34]

It is clear from this example that the reconciliation process can be rewarding, difficult, liberating, and painful. It is important to stay on the path of reconciliation. As the quote at the beginning of this essay reminds us, "We are runaway slaves from our own past, and only by turning to face the hounds can we find our freedom beyond them." Let us continue to seek freedom through racial reconciliation.

Discussion Questions

1. The "little people" as Governor Faubus referred to them, were losing their "southern way of life." What do you think they actually gave up in the process of public school integration?

2. This essay recounts the experiences of two victims of racial intolerance, Elizabeth Eckford and Hazel Bryan Massery. What were the immediate consequences of racial intolerance for each of these women? What were the longterm consequences of racial intolerance for each of these women?

3. What are your perceptions of the racial reconciliation process? In what ways did Hazel Bryan Massery and Elizabeth Eckford live up to your perceptions of the process? In what ways could your congregation assist in the racial reconciliation process? In what ways could you assist in the racial reconciliation process?

4. What are some elements of white privilege that whites seem to assume but are unable to acknowledge or even to see?

5. What are the spiritual risks to blacks and whites engaged in the racial reconciliation process?

More Books about Little Rock

Harry S. Ashmore, *Civil Rights and Wrongs: A Memoir of Race and Politics, 1944–1996* (Columbia, South Carolina: University of South Carolina Press, 1997).

Baer, Frances Lisa Baer. *Resistance to Public School Desegregation: Little Rock and Beyond* (New York: LFB Scholarly Publishing, 2008).

Daisy Bates, *The Long Shadow of Little Rock: A Memoir, with a New Preface by William B. Gatewood, Jr, reprint edition* (Fayetteville, Arkansas: University of Arkansas Press, 1987).

Melba Patillo Beals, *Warriors Don't Cry: A Searing Memoir of the Battle to Integrate Little Rock's Central High* (New York: Washington Square Press, 1995).

Melba Patillo Beals, *White Is a State of Mind: A Memoir* (New York: G. P. Putnam's Sons, 1999).

Virgil T. Blossom, *It HAS Happened Here* (New York: Harper, 1959).

Will Counts, *A Life Is More Than a Moment: The Desegregation of Little Rock's Central High*. Introduction by Will Campbell, Essays by Ernest Dumas and Robert S. McCord (Bloomington, Indiana: Indiana University Press, 1999, 2007).

Orval Faubus, *Down from the Hills, II* (Little Rock, Arkansas: Democrat Printing & Lithographic Company, 1985).

Elizabeth Huckaby, *Crisis at Central High, Little Rock, 1957–58*. Forward by Harry Ashmore (Baton Rouge, Louisiana: Louisiana State University Press, 1980).

Elizabeth Jacoway and Fred C. Williams, Eds. *Understanding the Little Rock Crisis: An Exercise in Remembrance and Reconciliation* (Fayetteville, Arkansas: University of Arkansas Press, 1999).

Jay Jennings, *Carry the Rock: Race, Football, and the Soul of an American City* (New York: Rodale, 2010).

John A Kirk, *Redefining the Color Line: Black Activism in Little Rock, Arkansas, 1940–1970* (Gainesville, Florida: University of Florida Press, 2002).

Mackie O'Hara and Alex Richardson, Eds. *Beyond Central, Toward Acceptance: A Collection of Oral Histories from Students of Little Rock Central High* (Little Rock, Arkansas: Butler Center Books, Butler Center for Arkansas Studies, Central Arkansas Library System, 2009).

Roy Reed, *Faubus: The Life and Times of an American Prodigal* (Fayetteville, Arkansas: University of Arkansas Press, 1997).

Beth Roy, *Bitters in the Honey: Tales of Hope and Disappointment across Divides of Race and Time* (Fayetteville, Arkansas: University of Arkansas Press, 1999).

Grif Stockley, *Daisy Bates: Civil Rights Crusader from Arkansas* (Jackson, Mississippi: University Press of Mississippi, 2005).

Notes

I am indebted to Dr. Jerry Taylor, associate professor of Bible, Missions, and Ministry at Abilene Christian University, who encouraged me to pursue this topic. His faithful friendship and wise counsel are continuous sources of inspiration and strength. I am also grateful to Dr. Jessie Carney Smith, Dean of the Library and Camille Cosby Distinguished Chair in the Humanities at Fisk University, whose lectures forty-five years ago ignited my interest in African American history, expanding my horizons immeasurably. This paper is based on presentations made at the Racial Unity Leadership Summit, Sycamore View Church of Christ, January 16 2015, and Harding School of Theology, February 26 2015.

[1] Timothy B. Tyson, *Blood Done Sign My Name: A True Story* (NY: Three Rivers Press, 2004), 307.

[2] "Little Rock Central High School National Historic Site," The Encyclopedia of Arkansas History and Culture. accessed February 10, 2016, http://www.encyclopediaofarkansas.net/.

[3] America's Black Holocaust Museum, dedicated to victims of the enslavement of Africans in the United States, was founded in Milwaukee by James Cameron, the nation's only known survivor of a lynching. The museum building closed in 2008, reopening as a virtual exhibit in 2012. accessed February 10, 2016, http://www.abhmuseum.org/.

[4] Quoted in Elizabeth Jacoway, *Turn Away Thy Son: Little Rock, The Crisis that Shocked the Nation* (New York: Free Press, 2007), 48. The Brown decision outlawed separate educational facilities for blacks and whites as inherently unequal. School systems, subsequently, began planning for integration in order to comply with court orders. Such plans, along with reactionary opposition to them, came to influence virtually every phase of contemporary life, especially in the southeast with its history of slavery, rebellion, and racial repression.

[5] Jacoway, 101–02.

[6] Jacoway, 114.

[7] Jacoway, 69.

[8] Jacoway, 120, 137, 162. Segregationist ministers, unlike their counterparts in mainline denominations, had access to people capable of violence and, therefore presumably, influence with violence-prone individuals; and Ernest Q. Campbell and Thomas F. Pettigrew, *Christians in Racial Crisis: A Study of Little Rock's Ministry* (Washington, DC: Public Affairs Press, 1959), 61.

[9] Jacoway, 7; and Karen Anderson, *Little Rock: Race and Resistance at Central High School* (Princeton, New Jersey: Princeton University Press, 2010), 1–3.

[10] Carlotta Walls LaNier, *A Mighty Long Way: My Journey to Justice at Little Rock Central High School* (New York: One World Books, 2009), 58–59. In *Lessons from Little Rock*, Terrence Roberts, another of the Nine, wrote, "The school board, in deference to the fears expressed by white citizens in Little Rock that we would become socially (read sexually) involved with the white students, had required the nine of us to sign an affidavit that we would not engage in any extracurricular activities at Central, so we hung out with our former Horace Mann schoolmates. We went to dances and parties at Mann, and continued to see our friends socially and at church. They were part of a significant group of people who gave us unqualified support and encouragement." (Little Rock, Arkansas: Butler Center Books, Butler Center for Arkansas Studies, Central Arkansas Library System, 2009), 122.

[11] Roberts, who later earned a degree in social work and a PhD in psychology, wrote, "I was afraid. I had never been that afraid at any other time in my life. Fear was a major part of my daily existence . . . . Fear is portable; you can take it with you wherever you go. But I did not have to let fear become a barrier to my going to school . . . . I knew that racial discrimination was wrong. Nobody had to tell me that. I also knew that it bordered on the criminal to deny basic rights to people simply because they happened to have black skin . . . . I saw fear as simply part of the price I had to pay, part of a down payment on a life free of racial discrimination" (Roberts, *Lessons from Little Rock*), 88; and Anderson, Little Rock, 108–09.

[12] Jacoway, 214–241; and David Margolick, *Elizabeth and Hazel: Two Women of Little Rock* (New Haven, CT: Yale University Press, 2011), 114, 187, 271. On the harassment of Minniejean Brown and her reactions, see Anderson, Little Rock, 94–96, 109–10, 115–18.

[13] LaNier, 118–19.

[14] David Margolick. "Through A Lens, Darkly." Vanity Fair, 2007. accessed April 11, 2016, http://www.vanityfair.com/news/2007/09/littlerock200709/.

[15] Ibid.

[16] Elizabeth Jacoway, *Turn Away Thy Son: Little Rock, the Crisis That Shocked the Nation* (Simon and Schuster, 2007).; Ravi Perry, and D. LaRouth Perry. *The Little Rock Crisis: What Desegregation Politics Says About Us* (New York: Springer, 2015).

[17] Margolick, 162, 164.

[18] Margolick, 135, 145–47.

[19] Margolick, 166, 185, 261.

[20] "Orval Faubus: The Mike Wallace Interview." accessed March 30, 2016. http://www .hrc.utexas.edu/multimedia/video/2008/wallace/faubus_orval_t.html.

[21] For more information, see "The Lost Year || About The Lost Year." accessed March 30, 2016, http://www.thelostyear.com/.

[22] New state anti-integration laws, designed to give segregationists unprecedented legal power, facilitated the referendum of 27 September 1958. See Sondra Gordy, *Finding the Lost Year: What Happened When Little Rock Closed Its Public Schools* (Fayetteville, Arkansas: University of Arkansas Press, 2009), 50. Five board members resigned simultaneously; segregationist Dale Alford had resigned previously in order to challenge Brooks Hays for United States Congress. Hays, a sitting congressman, had sought unsuccessfully to avert confrontation between federal and state authorities. He defeated rabid segregationist Amis Guthridge in the democratic primary but lost to Alford in the general election.

[23] Jacoway, 60.

[24] Wayne Upton, "Love of God and Neighbor Can Weld Us into a Strong Nation and Banish Governmental Corruption," undated news clipping, Paul M. Tucker Papers, Center for Restoration Studies, Milliken Special Collections and Archives, Abilene Christian University Library; "Eisenhower Administration. Wayne Upton. Columbia University, Oral History Research Office, 1973," University of Arkansas at Little Rock, Center for Arkansas History and Culture, Collections and Archives, fiche 14; and "Interview with Wayne Upton," UALR, Center for Arkansas History and Culture, Collections and Archives, UALR-ORH-0258.

[25] Anderson, *Little Rock*, 173; Gordy, *Finding the Lost Year*, 14, 38; and John A. Kirk, *Beyond Little Rock: The Origins and Legacies of the Central High Crisis* (New York: Free Press, 2007), 96.

[26] Quoted in Gordy, 69.

[27] Cartwright reached far beyond the traditional roles of a local pastor, working behind the scenes to expand inter-racial dialogue through the Arkansas Council on Human Relations, the Little Rock Conference on Religion and Race, and the Southern Regional Council. He emerged as a national spokesman on Christianity and race, having written for *Christian Century, Christianity and Crisis, The Progressive, New South*, and *The Reporter*, and was awarded an honorary doctorate by TCU in 1976.

[28] Margolick, 185, 211–12, 227.

[29] Margolick, 201–02.

[30.] David Margolick, Elizabeth and Hazel.

[31.] David Margolick. "Through A Lens, Darkly."

[32] Margolick, David. "Elizabeth Eckford and Hazel Bryan: The Story behind the Photograph That Shamed America," October 8, 2011, sec. World. http://www.telegraph .co.uk/news/worldnews/northamerica/8813134/Elizabeth-Eckford-and-Hazel-Bryan-the -story-behind-the-photograph-that-shamed-America.html.

[33] Ibid.

[34] Ibid.

Reflections on Civil Rights and the White Churches of Christ

by Richard T. Hughes

THE FAILURES OF WHITE CHURCHES OF CHRIST WITH RESPECT TO racial equality were immense during the period of America's Freedom Movement, but there seems no point—and it would not serve us well—to recount those failures today. If you want to read about those failures, I refer you to the excellent summary essay by Douglas Foster in a book edited by Gary Holloway and John York in 2002—*Unfinished Reconciliation*. Or the marvelous book by Wes Crawford, *Shattering the Illusion: How African American Churches of Christ Moved from Segregation to Independence*. Or even the chapter on black/white relations during the time of the Freedom Movement in my own book, *Reviving the Ancient Faith*.

But while it will not serve us well to recount those failures today, what will serve us well is to inquire into the *reasons* for those failures. What caused and sustained those failures on the ground were deep and far-reaching theological failures, and if we hope to be faithful to the biblical text, those are the failures we now must address.

85

I offer these reflections not to condemn the dead, but rather to lift up the hope that if we can take stock of the theological failures that undermined the purposes of the kingdom of God in this small corner of the Christian world over fifty years ago, perhaps in our time, in this time, we can do better.

I offer these reflections in the hope that future preachers will embrace the great biblical themes of justice and reconciliation.

And I offer these reflections in the hope that they will not only embrace those themes but will preach them and act on them in courageous ways.

But make no mistake: any pulpit minister who wants to proclaim what the Bible actually says about justice and mercy and reconciliation must summon enormous amounts of courage, especially in our time when the nation has returned to the politics of race and class and when the racial and economic divides in the United States are, in many respects, as great as they were over fifty years ago.

The Seductive Power of the Dominant Culture

The great similarity between our time and that time leads us directly to the first observation I want to make today, and it is this: our fathers and mothers in the days of the Freedom Movement read the biblical text through the lens of the dominant culture. But we must find a way to read the dominant culture through the lens of the biblical text. Indeed, we must find a way to read the dominant culture through the lens of the kingdom of God

In the very first of the fourteen films in the "Eyes on the Prize" series that documents America's Civil Rights years, a white woman from Montgomery, Alabama, Virginia Durr, offers these perceptive words.

> If you're born into a system that's wrong—whether it's a slave system or a segregated system—you take it for granted. And I was born into a system that was segregated and denied blacks the right to vote—also denied women the right to vote. And I took it for granted. Nobody told me any different. Nobody said it was strange or unusual.[1]

At one level, Virginia Durr's comment helps explain the behavior of Churches of Christ just as it helps explain the behavior of Baptists, Methodists,

Presbyterians and scores of other white denominations during the years of the Freedom Movement, for all had been shaped by the defining power of the dominant culture on the question of race. Like Durr, they all took that culture for granted.

Further, Durr's comment opens a window on the incredibly seductive power of *any* dominant culture, for the dominant culture invariably seeks to define us, to shape us, and to mold us into its image. This is why Durr said of the racial culture of the American South during the 1950s and 1960s, "I took it for granted. Nobody told me any different." And that is why Scripture candidly speaks of the values of the dominant culture as "the powers of this dark world" and "the spiritual forces of evil in the heavenly realms" whose values are sustained by "the rulers" and "the authorities" of the present age.

The question for Christians, then, is both simple and clear: how can we resist? I know of no way to resist the shaping and defining power of the dominant culture unless we possess two assets. First, we must occupy a vantage point that allows us to look into our culture, as it were, from outside the culture itself. And second, that vantage point must provide us with a set of values that are foreign to the culture, that stand in judgment on the culture, and that challenge the culture's values in radical ways.

Resisting the Sirens of Our Culture: Embracing the Gospel of Grace

The fact is that every Christian has access to precisely that sort of vantage point. The New Testament describes that vantage point with the simple word, *gospel*—the good news that God loves us infinitely more than we can fathom, has accepted us, and has said "yes" to us in spite of our inevitable failures, our brokenness, and our sins.

That is the gospel message, the heart of biblical faith. But there is a corollary to this central message—a corollary to which the New Testament writers return time and again. No one puts it better than John in his first epistle:

> We know love by this, that he laid down his life for us—and we
> ought to lay down our lives for one another. How does God's
> love abide in anyone who has the world's goods and sees a

brother or sister in need and yet refuses help? Little children, let us love, not in word or speech, but in truth and action. (3:16–18)

So the gospel message has two components. First, God extends his radical, self-giving love and grace to each of us, has accepted us, and has said "yes" to us in spite of our inevitable failures, our brokenness, and our sins. And second, God's love requires that we extend love and grace to others and say "yes" to them in spite of their inevitable failures, brokenness, and sin. The first component—God's own love and grace—is the driving, enabling power behind the second component, the grace we must extend to our neighbors.

But what happens when a Christian tradition seldom preaches the gospel of God's free and unmerited grace? What happens when a Christian tradition identifies God's grace with God's commands? What happens when a Christian tradition defines the "plan of salvation" not in terms of what God has done for us but rather in terms of the human response to divine commands?

What happens is this—that the Christian tradition that fails to proclaim God's unmerited grace has severed the driving force behind the love and grace that, according to the gospel message, we must extend to others.

And that is precisely what happened in Churches of Christ for a period of a hundred and fifty years—from the 1820s when Churches of Christ first began to identify God's grace with God's commands to the 1970s when Churches of Christ finally discovered and widely preached the good news of God's unmerited grace.

A single story will help us see the issue. By the 1930s, there were few preachers among Churches of Christ who proclaimed a message of "unmerited grace." One of those was K. C. Moser, a native Texan and a preacher in Oklahoma and Texas from the 1920s through the 1970s. A careful reading of his Bible convinced Moser that God's grace was to be found not in his commands but in the cross of Christ. He published his views in 1932 in a book he entitled *The Way of Salvation*.

But it was not until 1934, when he published an article in the Texas-based *Firm Foundation*, that Churches of Christ paid any serious regard to his perspective. The response, when it came, was almost entirely negative.

Quite simply, Moser argued that while baptism and good works were important, the gospel was a message of unmerited grace and the proper response to that grace was trust in Christ who had been "crucified, buried, and raised for our justification." The editor of the *Firm Foundation*, G. H. P. Showalter, rejected Moser's claim out of hand and pressed him to "speedily abandon such fantastic speculation."[2]

A storm of controversy quickly erupted over Moser's emphasis on unmerited grace and he became *persona non grata* in many quarters of Churches of Christ for the next forty years.

And when the Freedom Movement emerged in the mid-1950s, Churches of Christ almost entirely lacked the vantage point that might have allowed them to bring to that moment the insights of John: "How does God's love abide in anyone who has the world's goods and sees a brother or sister in need and yet refuses help?" Indeed, they almost entirely lacked the vantage point that might have prompted them to extend unmerited grace to their neighbors just as God had extended his unmerited grace to them.

Resisting the Sirens of Our Culture: Embracing the Gospel of the Kingdom

In addition to the gospel of grace, the New Testament offers Christians another vantage point from which we can resist the sirens of the dominant culture. Matthew describes that vantage point as "the gospel of the kingdom." Here are his words in chapter four:

> Jesus went throughout Galilee, teaching in their synagogues and proclaiming the good news [i.e., *the gospel*] of the kingdom and healing every disease and every sickness among the people (4:23).

Matthew's phrase, "the gospel of the kingdom," offers an early introduction to a theme that resonates throughout the gospels, namely, "the kingdom of God." And if we inquire into the meaning of the kingdom of God, the answer is not hard to find.

In virtually every instance where the phrase, "kingdom of God," appears in the New Testament, it is closely linked to concern for the poor, the dispossessed, those in prison, the maimed, the lame, the blind, and all those who suffer at the hands of the world's elites. In other words, the kingdom of God is where the powerless are empowered, where the hungry are fed, where the sick are healed, where the poor are sustained, and where those who find themselves marginalized by the rulers of this world are finally offered equality and justice.

Put another way, the "gospel of the kingdom of God" is the corollary to the "gospel of grace." It tells us that just as God has said "yes" to us in spite of our failures, so we must say "yes" to others in spite of their failures. Or, in the words of John, "We know love by this, that he laid down his life for us—and we ought to lay down our lives for one another" (I John 3:16).

We don't have time to explore the idea of the kingdom of God in the biblical text in great detail, but a handful of New Testament passages will help us grasp the point.

In the second chapter of Luke, an angel appears to shepherds in the field by night and proclaims, "good news of great joy for all the people: [for] to you is born this day in the city of David a Savior, who is the Messiah, the Lord."

In the context of imperial Rome, the angel's proclamation was both revolutionary and seditious, for its two key words—Savior and Lord—were titles routinely applied to the emperor Caesar Augustus. Indeed, Caesar's titles included "Divine," "Son of God," "God," "God from God," "Redeemer," "Liberator," "Lord," and "Savior of the World."

"[Early] Christians must have understood," John Dominic Crossan concludes, "that to proclaim Jesus as Son of God was deliberately denying Caesar his highest title and that to announce Jesus as Lord and Savior was calculated treason."[3]

So when that angel proclaimed to the shepherds the birth of the One who was Savior and Lord, the angel offered the shepherds a vantage point that allowed them to look into their culture, as it were, from outside the culture itself and a vantage point that offered the shepherds a set of values that challenged their culture in radical ways.

It is one thing to proclaim that Jesus is Savior and Lord, but it is something else to ask what that Savior and Lord requires, and that is the question that Luke answers with incredible clarity in Luke, chapter three—a passage that contrasts the humble kingdom of God with the all-pervasive power and splendor of the Roman Empire. Luke sets up the contrast beautifully, referring first to the ruling elites of his day.

> In the fifteenth year of the reign of Emperor Tiberius—when
> Pontius Pilate was governor of Judea, and Herod was tetrarch of
> Galilee, and his brother Philip tetrarch of the region of Ituraea
> and Trachonitis, and Lysanias tetrarch of Abilene, during the
> high priesthood of Annas and Caiaphas, the word of God came
> . . . . (3:1–2)

Came to whom? It came, Luke tells us, "to John son of Zechariah in the wilderness." Here, Luke subtly contrasts the wilderness where John resided with the imperial courts of Tiberius Caesar, Herod, Philip, and Lysanias. Later in his Gospel, Luke was not so subtle, since he reports that Jesus himself contrasted John's poverty with the luxury of imperial power. "What then did you go out to see?" Jesus asked the people. "Someone dressed in soft robes? Look, those who put on fine clothing and live in luxury are in royal palaces. What then did you go out to see? A prophet? Yes, I tell you, and more than a prophet" (7:26).

Tellingly, Matthew draws a very similar contrast. After reporting that the imperial powers—notably Herod and Archelaus—sought to murder the child who was savior and lord, Matthew offers this simple but stunning sentence: "In those days John the Baptist came, preaching in the wilderness of Judea." And the point Matthew clearly makes is that unlike Herod and Archelaus, John was not a product of royal palaces but of the wilderness where, in fact, he wore clothing of camel's hair, and a leather belt around his waist; and his food was locust and wild honey (3:4). The contrast Matthew draws between John, on the one hand, and the imperial rulers, on the other, could not have been greater.

Finally, what message did John proclaim? Did he preach the American gospel that "God helps those who help themselves?" Hardly. According to Luke, John preached a message of radical compassion for those in need. And when the crowds asked him, "What then should we do?" John replied, 'Anyone who has two shirts should share with the one who has none; and anyone who has food should do the same'" (3:10–11).

The point is this—that John the Baptist, both through the life he lived and the message he preached, offered those around him a vantage point that allowed them to look into their culture, as it were, from outside the culture and allowed them to claim a set of values that would challenge the culture in radical ways.

And Jesus did the very same thing when he came to Nazareth and there, in the synagogue, announced his mission and his vocation. According to Luke,

> He went to Nazareth, where he had been brought up, and on the Sabbath day he went into the synagogue, as was his custom. He stood up to read, and the scroll of the prophet Isaiah was handed to him. Unrolling it, he found the place where it is written:
>
> > The Spirit of the Lord is on me,
> > > because he has anointed me
> > > to proclaim good news to the poor.
> > He has sent me to proclaim freedom for the prisoners
> > > and recovery of sight for the blind,
> > to set the oppressed free,
> > > to proclaim the year of the Lord's favor.
>
> Then he rolled up the scroll, gave it back to the attendant and sat down. The eyes of everyone in the synagogue were fastened on him. He began by saying to them, "Today this scripture is fulfilled in your hearing" (4:16–21).

The gospels record only one other instance when Jesus defined the concerns that would characterize his mission and vocation. Matthew reports that John the Baptist, languishing in prison, heard of the work Jesus was doing and "sent word by his disciples and said to him, 'Are you the one who is to come, or are we to wait for another?'" And Jesus replied, "Go and tell John what you hear and see: the blind receive their sight, the lame walk, the lepers are cleansed, the deaf hear, the dead are raised, and the poor have good news brought to them."

By framing his mission and vocation in these terms, Jesus lined out the contours of what he often called "the kingdom of God." And that kingdom provided then—and still provides—a transcendent point of reference that allows Jesus' followers in every time and place to look into their culture, as it were, from outside the culture and to claim a transcendent set of values that can challenge the culture in radical ways.

Numerous other passages flesh out this vision of the kingdom of God. In Luke, for example, those who are first—the rich and the powerful—will be last, while those who are last—the poor and oppressed—will be first (13:29–30). Only those who are humble like little children can enter the kingdom of God (18:16–17). And Luke reports Jesus' comment, "How hard it is for the rich to enter the kingdom of God" (18:24).

And in the only full description of the final judgment that shows up in the biblical text, Jesus explains what is required for entry into the kingdom of God. Remarkably, there is nothing here that even remotely hints at the various orthodoxies that Christians of virtually all persuasions have erected over the years. Instead, the message is simple and clear and focuses on one simple question: What did you do for people who are poor, hungry, marginalized, and oppressed?

> "Come, you who are blessed by my Father," Jesus said, "Take your inheritance, the kingdom prepared for you since the creation of the world. For I was hungry and you gave me something to eat, I was thirsty and you gave me something to drink, I was a stranger and you invited me in, I needed clothes and you clothed me, I was sick and you looked after me, I was in prison and you came to visit me." (Matt. 25:34–40)

All these stories shed ever more light on that vantage point called the kingdom of God from which we could—if we would—challenge the dominant culture in radical ways.

The Churches of Christ and the Kingdom of God

But in the 1950s and 1960s—the years of America's Freedom Movement— Churches of Christ, like virtually all the churches in the American South, almost entirely failed to claim that vantage point and to occupy its high and transcendent ground. As a result, they were captives of the dominant culture, captives who failed to gain a biblical perspective on the great struggle of their time. And without that perspective—without that vantage point called the kingdom of God—they were powerless to speak or act in biblical and prophetic ways on behalf of people who, because of the color of their skin, had been marginalized and oppressed throughout the course of American history.

Ironically, the people who waged that struggle for equal rights, for equal housing, for equal access to food, education, and clothing—ironically, these were some of the people Jesus clearly envisioned when he said, "He has anointed me to bring good news to the poor . . . and . . . let the oppressed go free." These were some of the people John the Baptist envisioned when he said, "Whoever has two coats must share with anyone who has none; and whoever has food must do likewise." And these are some of the people Jesus envisioned when he laid down the requirements for entry into the Kingdom of God: Did you feed me? Did you clothe me? Did you slake my thirst and care for me when I was in prison? For if you did it for the least of these, you did it to me.

But Churches of Christ typically failed to make that connection and, as a result, they took their place alongside those other southern churches of whom Martin Luther King spoke in his "Letter from a Birmingham Jail" when he wrote,

> In the midst of blatant injustices inflicted upon the Negro, I
> have watched white churches stand on the sidelines and merely
> mouth pious irrelevancies and sanctimonious trivialities. In the
> midst of a mighty struggle to rid our nation of racial and eco-
> nomic injustice, I have heard so many ministers say, "Those are
> social issues with which the gospel has no real concern."[4]

And then he continued:

> I have traveled the length and breadth of Alabama, Mississippi
> and all the other southern states. On sweltering summer days
> and crisp autumn mornings I have looked at her beautiful
> churches with their lofty spires pointing heavenward. I have

beheld the impressive outlay of her massive religious education buildings. Over and over again I have found myself asking: "What kind of people worship here? Who is their God?"[4]

The Root of the Problem

And now we must ask, what was it about Churches of Christ that prevented them from connecting the Freedom Movement of the 1950s and 1960s to the biblical vision of the kingdom of God?

We have already noted that Churches of Christ had obscured from an early date the biblical witness regarding God's unmerited grace which empowers the followers of Jesus to extend unmerited grace to their neighbors.

But there is more—so much more.

It was surely not the case that Churches of Christ were unfamiliar with the Bible, for the Bible has been the singular focus of Churches of Christ from the time of their inception in the early nineteenth century.

But it is the case that Churches of Christ forced questions and concerns onto the biblical text that, at best, were marginal to the biblical witness. And it is also the case that Churches of Christ read the Bible in ways that simply obscured its vision of the kingdom of God.

Alexander Campbell set the agenda for Churches of Christ when he vigorously promoted a restoration of primitive Christianity. The problem was not with the idea of restoration in its own right since the notion of restoration is an inherently useful vision. The problem lay in the fact that Campbell, indebted as he was to the principles of the Age of Reason, defined restoration and the kingdom of God in broadly constitutional and institutional terms rather than as a theological or ethical treatise. Instead, Campbell viewed the New Testament more as a scientific manual upon which rational and unbiased people might reconstruct in scientifically precise way the forms and structures of the primitive church.

The notion of forms and structures is crucial to this conversation, for Campbell seldom asked what the Bible said about the poor. Instead, he asked about the biblical pattern for corporate assemblies. He seldom asked what the Bible said about marginalized people. Instead, he asked about a rationally constructed plan of salvation. He seldom asked what the Bible said about people oppressed by imperial powers. Instead, he asked about the biblical model for the proper organization of the local church. In all these ways, Campbell focused on restoring a cluster of practices that imparted to Churches of Christ their unique identity, but unfortunately, this concentration on precise practice deeply underplayed a broader theological vision for the kingdom of God.

But there is more, for in his zeal to restore the forms and structures of the primitive church, Campbell argued that the Christian age began, not with the birth of Jesus but with the birth of the church, an event recorded in Acts, chapter two. Everything prior to Acts 2, he argued, rightly belonged to what he called the "Mosaic dispensation" which had no relevance for the grand task of restoring the primitive church. In effect, then, Campbell minimized the importance not only of the Hebrew Bible but also of the gospels. Over time, that action would essentially sever Churches of Christ from the biblical vision of the kingdom of God for one finds that vision especially in the Hebrew prophets and the teachings of Jesus.

But there is still more, for even in the lifetime of Campbell, some in Churches of Christ had transformed Campbell's goal of restoring the primitive church into a fixed and settled conviction that they had, in fact, restored the one true church and that, outside of that church, there could be no salvation. By the 1950s and 1960s, the notion that one's salvation depended on one's belonging to the one true church had become for many members and congregations in this tradition the most important consideration of all.

Indeed, the vision of the one true church became so all-consuming that many identified the kingdom of God with the one true church, now restored to the earth. Some even argued that it was wrong to repeat that portion of the Lord's Prayer that says, "Thy kingdom come," for the kingdom had come when the church was established on the day of Pentecost in the first century and then again when Alexander Campbell and his comrades restored to the earth the one true church in the early nineteenth century.

When push came to shove, therefore, the contest between the kingdom of God, on the one hand, and the one true church, on the other, was decided before it began, for the theology of the one true church had swallowed the theology of the kingdom of God.

As far as the Freedom Movement is concerned, the bottom line is this— having obscured both the gospel of grace and the gospel of the kingdom, the white Churches of Christ were wholly unprepared to embrace their brothers and sisters of color who asked for nothing more than the things of which Jesus spoke in Matthew 25 when he said, "I was hungry and you gave me food, I was thirsty and you gave me something to drink, I was a stranger and you welcomed me, I was naked and you gave me clothing, I was sick and you took care of me, I was in prison and you visited me." They were wholly unprepared to discern in that movement the faces of those of whom John wrote, "How does God's love abide in anyone who has the world's goods and sees a brother or sister in need and yet refuses help?" Indeed, they were wholly unprepared to discern in the Freedom Movement the faces of the kingdom of God.

Trading the Kingdom of God for Christian America

But there is one more component in this story that we must not omit. There was a time when Churches of Christ nurtured a vibrant vision of the kingdom of God. Those who carried that vision were people like Barton Stone and David Lipscomb. But in due time, the seductive sirens of American nationalism drove that vision out of Churches of Christ and successfully replaced it with the notion that the United States was, in fact, a Christian nation and perhaps even the kingdom of God.

Those who labored under that conviction could only regard the cause of the Freedom Movement as an unjustified complaint, for how could this Christian nation have possibly denied equal rights and equal opportunity to any of its people? Martin Luther King and those for whom he spoke were, therefore, nothing more than agitators, inspired more by Communism than by anything resembling the Christian faith to which King so often appealed. A letter from Reuel Lemmons, editor of the *Firm Foundation*, to Jennings Davis, dean of students at Pepperdine University, makes this point unmistakably clear. "A lot of people wanted to compare Martin Luther King to Jesus Christ," Lemmons wrote. But "in reality,"

King was a modernist, and denied faith in Jesus Christ as taught in the Bible. . . . If he was not an outright Communist, he certainly advocated Communist causes. His absolute disregard for law and order except those laws and orders which he wanted to obey leaves me cold. . . . J. Edgar Hoover branded King as a notorious liar and Harry Truman said he was a troublemaker. This kind of man, black or white, I cannot conscientiously praise.[5]

Conclusions

I offer these reflections not to condemn the dead, but rather to lift up the hope that if we can take stock of the theological failures that undermined the purposes of the kingdom of God in this small corner of the Christian world over fifty years ago, perhaps in our time, in this time, we can do better.

And we have done better. We have been preaching the gospel of grace in a serious way for some forty or fifty years, and that is the message that has prompted and sustained the good work of racial reconciliation, first at Abilene Christian University and now here at Lipscomb University and in many congregations of our fellowship.

But there is so much more that must be done, so many bridges yet to be built, so many conversations still to be had, so many apologies that still must be offered, so much forgiveness that must be extended, and so many tears of repentance that still must be shed.

Beyond all of that, there is so much work still to be done to lift up the fallen, to stand with the oppressed, to support the marginalized, to feed the hungry, to clothe the naked, to visit those in prison, and to liberate those who have been imprisoned unjustly.

All of this is the legitimate work of the kingdom of God on earth.

But we will never accomplish this work until we embrace the gospel of Christ as the singular vantage point from which we can view and judge the sirens of our culture.

We will never accomplish this work until we embrace the values of the kingdom of God as the standard for our lives.

And as a fellowship committed to the call of God, Churches of Christ will never accomplish this work unless we allow the gospel of grace and the gospel of the kingdom to define us, to shape us, and to mold us. For only through the gospel will we find the power to respond as we should to those Jesus called "the least of these."

Discussion Questions

1. How do you define grace? Why is grace important in race reconciliation work?

2. The author challenges us to juxtapose the rational construction of the church with the theological mandates of the church. Identify five scriptures that address each of the following issues:

    a. Poverty
    b. Acts of worship/corporate assemblies
    c. Oppressed people
    d. Plan of Salvation
    e. Oppression by Imperial powers
    f. Organization of the local church

3. Discuss ways in which you live out each of the identified scriptures.

Notes:

[1] "Awakenings," *Eyes on the Prize: America's Civil Rights Years 1954–1965*, Volume 1, directed by Judith Vecchione (PBS Video, 1987).

[2] For a discussion of the controversy between Moser and Showalter see John Mark Hicks, "K. C. Moser and Churches of Christ," accessed April 8 2016, http://johnmarkhicks.com/2008/05/15/k-c-moser-and-churches-of-christ/.

[3] John Dominic Crossan, *God and Empire: Jesus against Rome, Then and Now* (San Francisco: HarperSanFrancisco, 2007), 107–08 and 141.

[4] Martin Luther King. "Letter from Birmingham Jail." In *Gospel of Freedom, ed. Jonathan Rieder.* New York: Bloomsbury Press, 2013.

[5] Reuel Lemmons, in a letter to Jennings Davis dated May 23 1968 in John Allen Chalk files, Harding School of Theology library.

CONTEMPORARY
CHALLENGES

Unveiling Radical Love

A Theological Reflection on Radical Love in the Age of Ferguson

by Stanley Talbert

> *We should hope not for a colorblind society but instead for a world in which we can see each other fully, learn from each other, and do what we can to respond to each other with love. That was King's dream—a society that is capable of seeing each of us, as we are, with love. This is a goal worth fighting for.*[1]
>
> —Michelle Alexander

IN *ALL ABOUT LOVE*, BELL HOOK DESCRIBES A WORK OF ART THAT saved her from drowning in the sea of nihilism. "The declaration, 'The search for love continues even in the face of great odds,' was painted in bright colors."[2] On her way to work, she would see this painting everyday and it would give her hope to love and be loved beyond despair. The tragic part about hook's story takes place when a *construction* company "so callously covered up a powerful message about love."[3] In her disappointment, the construction company covered an inspirational, artistic painting with bland, white paint.

In many ways, hook's search for love provides a powerful framework and point of departure to speak about radical love. Individuals, communities, churches, and nations desiring to enact radical love are challenged to *unveil* the love behind the whitewashed walls painted by the social construction companies of our world. Cornel West states, "The work of radical love is breaking the back of fear."[4] The work of radical love demands for the unveiling of the social constructions of racism, sexism, classism, xenophobia, and Islamophobia. Until we break the back of these categories, people will be consumed by nihilism manifested in police brutality, mass incarceration, poverty, and death.

In thinking about the quest for radical love, citizens of the United States are challenged to unveil radical love in the age of Ferguson. For many, the horrendous murder of the unarmed teenager, Michael Brown, manifested the ways in which white supremacy attempts to cover the lives of black and brown peoples through hate and racism. Radical love attempts to cut through the fear, the lies, and conspiracies that cover the truth.

The "Ferguson Report" attempted to uncover false notions of professionalism within the Ferguson Police Department. In relation to the report, law professor and civil rights attorney Theodore Shaw states,

> As the Department of Justice report concluded: 1) "Ferguson's police and municipal court practices both reflect and exacerbate existing racial bias, including racial stereotypes"; 2) "Ferguson's own data establish clear racial disparities that adversely impact African Americans"; and 3) "[t]he evidence shows that discriminatory intent is part of the reason for these disparities." In summary, the Ferguson Report reveals a pattern or practice of unlawful conduct within the Ferguson Police Department that violates the First, Fourth, and Fourteenth amendments to the United States Constitution, and federal statutory law.[5]

The Ferguson Report indicates that the catastrophic murder of Michael Brown with impunity did not occur in a vacuum, but in a context conducive to lies and deceit. For Shaw, Ferguson is a symbol of America. For Minister Osagyefo Sekou, a St. Louis native who is a leader in the Fellowship of

Reconciliation, Ferguson is a link in an entire chain of a global phenomena.[6] In short, the scandal of Ferguson is everywhere.

What does it mean to unveil radical love in the age of Ferguson? Where is God and God's love in the midst of the shootings of so many of God's black and brown children? How do we claim radical love as a force for social change in the twenty-first century? This reflection seeks to shows how the work of radical love can uncover destructive forces that disable its transformative power. The theological component of this paper seeks to understand radical love in light of (1) the notion of God, (2) the self, (3) the neighbor, and (4) the socio-political.

Radical Love and the Notion of God

Following the acquittal of George Zimmerman for the killing of the teen-aged Trayvon Martin, Anthea Butler, a University of Pennsylvania Religious Studies professor, evoked author William Jones' query, *Is God a White Racist?*[7] In her article, "The Zimmerman Acquittal: America's Racist God," Butler writes,

> When George Zimmerman told Sean Hannity that it was God's will that he shot and killed Trayvon Martin, he was diving right into what most good conservative Christians in America think right now. Whatever makes them protected, safe, and secure, is worth it at the expense of the black and brown people they fear.[8]

Butler articulates the ways in which people like George Zimmerman hide their hate behind notions of God. How can the God of radical love be the same God that tells people like George Zimmerman to kill unarmed black and brown children?

In the early nineteenth century, the German philosopher and anthropologist Ludwig Feuerbach (1804–1872) suggested that the idea of God was merely a projection of the wishes or desires of the ruling class. Butler's critique suggests that as Zimmerman hides behind the language of God's will, he has, in fact, in a Feuerbachian fashion made god in a white image. This perspective stands in a long line of the black intellectual tradition that has constantly juxtaposed a supposed American white God against white America's praxis toward black and brown peoples.

In the wake of Jim and Jane Crow lynching, social reformist Ida B. Wells-Barnett makes a similar distinction between religious ideals and praxis. Wells-Barnett notes how the fear of black men committing "unspeakable crimes" against white women fueled the early activity of lynching in America. "For this reason," Wells-Barnett argues, "the Christian and moral forces are silent in the presence of the horrible barbarities alleged to be done in the name of woman."[9]

In the age of Ferguson, we must ask difficult questions. Who is God in an age where unarmed children can be shot in the streets with impunity? If the American God is synonymous with the God of the Bible, why should people believe in that God? Author Ta-Nehisi Coates makes a similar claim to Butler when he argues that America has never yet fully betrayed its God of injustice and racism.[10] Reflecting on his earlier years in Baltimore he writes,

> I could not retreat, as did so many, into the church and its mysteries. My parents rejected all dogmas. We spurned the holidays marketed by the people who wanted to be white. We would not stand for their anthems. We would not kneel before their God. And so I had no sense that any just God was on my side. "The meek shall inherit the earth" meant nothing to me. The meek were battered in West Baltimore, stomped out at Walbrook Junction, bashed up on Park Heights, and raped in the showers of the city jail.[11]

Butler, Wells, and Ta-Nehisi Coates all demonstrate the ways in which the notion of God can enable blindness towards the catastrophe that is taking place in this present age. Their voices tend toward radical love because they are in the work of unveiling the lies and scandals about the God of liberation. Although Coates is an atheist, his words tend toward radical love and they can be interpreted as type of apophatic theology, which describes God by negation. In this theological tradition, one speaks of God only in terms of what He is not rather than by presuming to define what God is.[12] In this light, we understand that the uncovering of lies, deceit, and hypocrisy as a function of theology and that this uncovering brings us toward truth.

What are some constructive ways of thinking about God and radical love in the context of Ferguson terror? In the *Fire Next Time*, author James Baldwin says, "If the concept of God has any validity or any use, it can only be to make us larger, freer, and more loving. If God cannot do this, then it is time we got rid of Him."[13] This is one of the most powerful statements about God and love because it points human beings toward ethical action. It is also a bold claim that necessitates love as a precondition for any meaning of God. As opposed to a God of oppression, hate, and murder, Baldwin's God enables all people to love, to be freer, and larger.

It is important to keep track of the god people worship in the age of Ferguson. People of radical love have the task of uncovering notions of god that stand in contradiction to the God of radical love.

Radical Love and the Self

"You can only be destroyed by believing that you really are what the white world calls a nigger. I tell you this because I love you, and please don't you ever forget it."

—James Baldwin[14]

The love of the self is not often found in the theological corpus of white theologians. However, it is impossible to have a radical love for neighbor, community, or others, without a radical love for oneself. Some people may be hesitant to speak of radical love and the self because it may tend toward egoism and narcissism. However, in an age where there is so much self-hate in black and brown communities, there is a desperate need for a radical self-love.

We must be cautious about theologies and philosophies that attend to the neighbor and the political without tending to the self. Emmanuel Levinas's notion of "the sacrificing of the self for the neighbor," must be taken with caution by communities who have always been sacrificed at the hands of the nation.[15] Black and brown people, especially those who are poor, have to persistently fight to love themselves in a world of schools, neighborhoods, fast-food restaurants, drug stores, liquor stores, and police officers that compete for their non-existence.

In a letter to his nephew, Baldwin conveys his desire for his nephew to have self-love in a world of inhumanity. He says,

> The details and symbols of your life have been deliberately con-structed to make you believe what white people say about you. Please try to remember that what they believe, as well as what they do and cause you to endure, does not testify to your inferi-ority but to their inhumanity and fear.[16]

The overt messages inherent in the social *constructions* of America have the ability to smother radical self-love in the same way that the construc-tion workers whitewashed over bell hook's work of art. The challenge for Baldwin's nephew is to uncover the true reality that these false symbols are masking—the reality that blacks are indeed human.

Baldwin's analysis of America in the context of his nephew is an inter-esting paradox. A key element in Baldwin's writings is his keen attention to the private-life. We could argue that the private-life is analogous to the self. Although a nation consists of individuals and communities, Baldwin often spoke to America as a self—a mythic person. Baldwin here is affirming the humanity of his nephew (self-love) while concomitantly exposing the inhu-manity (self-hate) of America. In short, America's self-hate is transferred to the black nieces and nephews of James Baldwin, and subsequently they are taught to hate themselves.

Malcolm X is incomparable in his radical love for black people. He concentrated his energy in ameliorating the psychological dimensions of black self-hate. Theologian James Cone states, "He transformed the way black people [thought] about themselves. He transformed Negroes into *black* people, and thereby created the black arts movements, black studies in colleges and universities, black power and black liberation theology."[17] Malcolm X understood integration and non-violent protest as ways to further perpetuate self-hate. Malcolm X says, "Respect me, or put me to death."[18] Without Malcolm X, the black people in America would have a larger deficit in self-love.

But what are we to say about Malcolm X's contemporary on the subject of self-love? Does Martin Luther King, Jr.'s love for others jettison his love for black folks? In his speech to high school students in Philadelphia, King makes statements that may be mistaken for the words of Malcolm X. He says,

> Number one in your life's blueprint should be a deep belief in your own dignity, your own worth, and your own somebodie-ness. Don't allow anybody to make you feel that you are nobody. Always feel that you count. Always feel that you have worth. And always feel that your life has ultimate significance. Now, that means that you should not be ashamed of your color. . . . But don't be ashamed of your color. Don't be ashamed of your biological features. Somehow you must be able to say in your own lives—and really believe it—"I am black but beautiful," and believe it in your heart.[19]

Like Baldwin speaking to his nephew, and Malcolm speaking to the souls of black folk, King speaks a message of self-love to high school students. He teaches them to love their bodies in a society that has "placed a stigma on the Negroes' color." King's theological orientation dictated that people should be loved because all people are created in the *imago dei*.

Black Lives Matter is the affirmation of black humanity in the age of Ferguson. It is a message of radical love towards black and brown people in a society that has exhibited radical hate towards them. Not only has it sought to unveil the negative constructions on black life, but it has also sought to uncover the veils placed on particular black lives. While Black Lives Matter has attempted to bring light to the injustices surrounding the murders of unarmed black people, it has also been critical of which black lives are mourned for, while others wither in silence. It has uncovered the constructions of racism, sexism, and misogyny through its hastags: #SayHerName and #AllBlackLivesMatter. There is profound power in the affirmation that #BlackLivesMatter.

In the wake of the Black Lives Matter, many have contended "All Lives Matter." Although the proclamation that all lives matter is true, it jettisons any real discussion on the ways in which black lives have been historically excluded from the democratic process. People who are quick to bolster the #AllLivesMatter hash tag over and against #BlackLivesMatter, should remember that black people (and women) were excluded from the Preamble of the United States Declaration of Independence of 1776. All men did not refer to all people. The 13th, 14th, and 15th amendments to the United States Constitution witness to the ways in which black lives have not been valued historically in the United States.

Baldwin, King, and Malcolm X show the ways in which black people need a radical self-love in a world of perpetual hate. The United States cannot expect the youth in Ferguson, Baltimore, and Chicago to love our nation when she has taught them to hate themselves. Black and brown people and our country need radical self-love.

Radical Love and the Neighbor

"Segregation, to use the terminology of the Jewish philosopher Martin Buber, substitutes an "I-it" relationship for an "I-thou" relationship and ends up relegating persons to the status of things. Hence segregation is not only politically, economically and sociologically unsound, it is morally wrong and sinful."

—*Martin Luther King*[20]

What does it mean to unveil the constructions that hinder radical love from flourishing between the self and the neighbor and between neighborhoods? In a culture where sameness is deified and difference is demonized, radical love is suffocated and choked. How do we allow the *pneumata* of difference to breathe when police brutality disables people of difference to breathe? When society inhales the spirit of white supremacy, it infects the lungs of difference with hate and racism.

In the line of Martin Buber, Martin Luther King, Jr., understood segregation to be sinful because it changes the person who is made in the *imago dei* into a thing. In his *Letter from Birmingham Jail*, King said,

Any law that uplifts human personality is just. Any law that degrades human personality is unjust. All segregation statutes

are unjust because segregation distorts the soul and damages
the personality. It gives the segregator a false sense of superiority
and the segregated a false sense of inferiority.[21]

Segregation was not just an interpersonal obstruction, but it was also an
inner, personal obstruction. King articulates that segregation is not a neutral fact of experience, but it was something brought about by *segregators.*

Just as segregation did not happen in a vacuum, neither did segregators choose to segregate in a vacuum. For many, it was the god of white
supremacy who divinely inspired segregation. In *The Violence of Desperate
Men*, King quotes letters written to him by the KKK saying, "God do not
intend the White People and the Negro to go to gather if he did we would
be the same."[22] This demonic theology was not only represented in King's
time but is heard in the writings of abolitionist and social reformer Fredrick
Douglass. In his essay, *What to the Slave Is the Fourth of July?*, Douglass jux-
taposes the celebration of American freedom with chattel slavery. He says,

> At the very moment that they are thanking God for the enjoy-
> ment of civil and religious liberty, and for the right to worship
> God according to the dictates of their own consciences, they are
> utterly silent in respect to a law which robs religion of its chief
> significance, and makes it utterly worthless to a world lying in
> wickedness.[23]

Douglass is critical of religion in the United States because it allows the same
God who liberates the United States to enslave black people. Slavery and Jim
and Jane Crow prevent human beings from seeing others as human beings.

Because Jim and Jane Crow is subsequent to chattel slavery in America,
it was a new form of racist theology that hindered radical love. Within
Cornel West's prophetic thought, he names key components that include:
discernment, connection (empathy), tracking hypocrisy, and hope. He
defines empathy as, "The capacity to get in contact with the anxieties and
frustrations of others."[24]

In many ways, West's emphasis on empathy gets at the tragic heart of
a society that can't step into the shoes of their neighbors. From slavery, to

Jim and Jane Crow, to Ferguson, white supremacist radical hate has blinded the prospect for radical love due to a lack of empathy. The same god who promotes slavery and lynching in the era of Jim and Jane Crow, is the same god who inspires the shooting and mass-incarceration of black and brown peoples. This diabolical theology hinders ethical action and love for one's neighbor; therefore, the God of love, justice, and peace must be reclaimed in the 21st century.

Radical Love and the Socio-Political

All dimensions of radical love are particularly important, but what about love on a socio-political horizon. How can radical love galvanize the Black Lives Matter revolutionary activity toward a powerful source for social transformation? What does love look like in this way?

As a secular humanist, Richard Rorty praises his grandfather Walter Rauschenbusch (despite the critiques of Reinhold Niebuhr) for taking Christianity beyond the personal to the social. Rorty states,

> Secular humanists like myself think of the doctrine of original sin as having, disastrously, diverted the attention of Christians from the needs of their neighbors to the state of their own souls. . . . Rauschenbusch urged us to think of Jesus as the successor of the Hebrew prophets, whose great theme—at least before the national catastrophe to which Jeremiah was reacting was social justice.[25]

Pointing to Rauschenbusch, Rorty highlights how Jesus carries the work of social justice from the Hebrew Prophets. Christianity should not be relegated to personal salvation, but it should focus on the self as well as the community, as well as society.

In thinking about love on a socio-political level, it may be difficult to find its place in a society where there is so much to be angry about. How can people in this generation maintain righteous indignation with a profound sense of radical love? bell hooks encounters this dissonance when she speaks about love in social justice movements. She says,

> When I travel around the nation giving lectures about ending
> racism and sexism, audiences, especially young listeners,
> become agitated when I speak about the place of love in any
> movement for social justice. Indeed, all the great movements
> for social justice in our society have strongly emphasized a love
> ethic. Yet young listeners remain reluctant to embrace the idea
> of love as a transformative force.[26]

hooks' encounter with younger listeners challenges them to have an ethic of radical love as a transformative force. She is right in noting the ways that love played important roles in social movements.

For King, Gandhi exemplified what is meant to enact the ethic of love on the social sphere. He says, "Gandhi was probably the first person in history to lift the love ethic of Jesus above mere interaction between individuals to a powerful and effective social force on a large scale."[27] Gandhi's nonviolent social action was not abstracted from his ethic love, and this was also true for King.

West describes King as a "revolutionary and radical Christian—a black Baptist minister and pastor whose intellectual genius and rhetorical power [was] deployed in the name of the Gospel of Jesus Christ."[28] He describes King's understanding in a way that goes beyond the personal ethic of love, but enables him to enact the gospel on a socio-political level through radical love.

In the age of Ferguson, it is easy to dismiss radical love as a social force. However, in the line with Baldwin, this love must be dangerous and take risks—far from sentimentalism. The radical hate that permeates our society in multivalent forms, tempts people to breathe in and embody hate. However, radical lovers must not be seduced by this hatred. While we are justified in hating white supremacy, the prison industrial complex, poverty, and racism, #BlackLivesMatter is challenged to keep radical love as its central moral compass.

Conclusion

*"I really mean that there was no love in the church.
It was a mask for hatred and self-hatred and despair."*

—James Baldwin[29]

As a theological student, ordained minister, and activist I am not only challenged to think about the ways that the God of liberation is active in the radical love of the self, of the neighbor, and the social-political. I am also interested in how the love of God is carried about by communities of faith and churches in particular. What is the church's role in the era of Ferguson?

Martin Luther King, Jr., struggled with black and white churches during the Civil Rights Movement. The former was dormant while the latter was silent in the face of oppression. Minister Sekou's message to clergy in Ferguson in his, "The Clergy's Place is with the Protestors in Ferguson," is similar to King's during the Civil Rights Movement. They both ask, "How can churches preach about radical love when they avoid the places that need it most?"

James Baldwin left the church because he couldn't find love in the church. The "mask" of the church prevented radical love to exist in the church for him. I believe that it is the task of ministers and faith leaders to help the church take off its myriad masks so that it can demonstrate the radical love of Christ in communities of radical catastrophe. It may be the *constructed* walls of our churches that have prevented radical love for overcoming racism. However, if the church exists as the body of Christ, then the radical love of the church must be for the world and not exist for itself.

Discussion Questions

1. What is your conception of radical love? What distinctions would you make between "radical love" and "love?"

2. How can individuals, communities, churches, and institutions embody radical love in the face of racism? What does this look like concretely?

3. What does "Black Lives Matter" mean to you? How can it be understood as a message of radical love? Is gospel of Jesus mutually exclusive from "Black Lives Matter?"

4. Martin Luther King, Jr., described segregation as sinful because it degraded the humanity of those who were being segregated. In what ways do you see segregation existing post the Jim Crow era? Whose humanity is being degraded and what tangible actions can be taken?

5. In the wake of the shooting of Michael Brown in Ferguson, Missouri (August 9, 2014), there have been multiple protests in the US and throughout the world to stop police brutality and the shooting of unarmed people. These protests have also called for the indictments of officers associated with the shootings. How might we understand these protests (and the organizations behind the protests) as a manifestation of radical love? What theological/ biblical examples could you draw on to reflect on protesting as a witness to the love of God?

Notes

[1] Michelle Alexander, *The New Jim Crow: Mass Incarceration in the Age of Colorblindness*, Revised edition (New York: The New Press, 2010), 244.

[2] bell hooks. *All about Love: New Visions*. (New York: Perennial, 2001) xv.

[3] Ibid., xvii.

[4] Cornel West, *Class Session 3: King The Beloved Community, Realizing Radical Love*, Union Theological Seminary, September 15, 2015.

[5] Theodore Shaw, *The Ferguson Report: United States Department of Justice, Civil Rights Division* (New York: The New Press, 2015), Ix.

[6] Osagyefo Sekou, *The Clergy's Place is with the Protestors in Ferguson* http://america .aljazeera.com/opinions/2014/11/ferguson-protestmovementreligious.html/. Osagyefo Sekou, Nov. 23, 2014. Founded in 1915, the Fellowship of Reconciliation is the oldest interfaith peace organization in this country.

[7] William R. Jones, *Is God A White Racist?: A Preamble to Black Theology* (Boston: Beacon Press, 1997).

[8] Anthea Butler, "The Zimmerman Acquittal: Americas Racist God, July 16, 2013," accessed March 16, 2016, http://religiondispatches.org/the-zimmerman-acquittal -americas-racist-god/.

[9] Barnett, Ida B., and Mia Bay, *The Light of Truth: Writings of an Anti-lynching Crusader*, 406. Ida B. Wells-Barnett (1862–1931), a social reformist, journalist, and anti-lynching crusader. For more information about Wells-Barnett, see Patricia Ann Schechter, *Ida B. Wells-Barnett and American Reform, 1880–1930, Gender and American Culture* (Chapel Hill: University of North Carolina Press, 2001), Rychetta N. Watkins, "The Southern Roots of Ida B. Wells-Barnett's Revolutionary Activism," *Southern Quarterly* 45,3 (Spring 2008): 108–26, Wilma Peebles-Wilkins and E. Aracelis Francis, "Two Outstanding Black Women in Social Welfare History: Mary Church Terrell and Ida B. Wells-Barnett," *Affilia* 5,4 (December 1, 1990): 87–100, doi:10.1177/088610999000500406; Ida B. Wells, *The Red Record* (Open Road Media, 2015); Ida B. Wells, *Crusade for Justice: The Autobiography of Ida B. Wells* (University of Chicago Press, 2013).

[10] Ta-nehisi Coates, *Between The World and Me* (New York, Penguin Random House, 2015), 6.

[11] Ibid., 28.

[12] Apophatic theology, also known as negative theology, is a "Negative Theology | Theopedia," accessed March 10, 2016, http://www.theopedia.com/negative-theology/.

[13] James Baldwin, *Collected Essays* (New York: Library of America, 1998) 314.

[14] Ibid., 291.

[15] Emmanuel Levinas, "Useless Suffering", in *Entre Nous: On Thinking-of-the-Other*, trans. Michael B Smith and Barbara Harshav (New York and Chichester: Columbia University Press, 1998), 91–101.

[16] Baldwin, *Collected Essays*, 291.

[17] James Cone, *Remembering Malcolm and Martin* (2013), in *The Diary of Malcolm X*, 1.

[18] Betty Shabazz, *By Any Means Necessary* (New York: Pathfinder Press, 1992) 115.

[19] Martin Luther King, *The Radical King*, ed., Cornel West. (Boston, Massachusetts: Beacon Press, 2015), 65–66.

[20] Ibid., 133.

[21] Ibid., 133.

[22] Ibid., 5.

[23] Fredrick Douglas, *What To the Slave Is the Fourth of July* (1852), 123.

[24] Cornel West, *Beyond Eurocentrism and Multiculturalism: Prophetic Thought in Postmodern Times* (Monroe, ME: Common Courage Press, 1993), 3.

[25] Walter Rauschenbusch (1861–1918) was an American theologian most recognized as a leader in the Social Gospel movement. Reinhold Niebuhr (1892–1971) was an American theologian, critical of the idealisms and utopias which included the Social Gospel associated with Walter Rauschenbusch. Niebuhr believed that no movement could absolutely diminish evil in the world, but people and movements can only do relative good in history. Richard Rorty (1931–2007) is considered an American pragmatist philosopher who opposed foundationalism, rejecting claims of absolute truth. His philosophy was more concerned with the usefulness of ideas in society as opposed to the their "truthfulness." See his essay "Buds That Never Opened," in Walter Rauschenbusch, *Christianity and the Social Crisis: In the 21st Century,* ed. Paul Rauschenbush (New York: HarperOne, 2007) 348.

[26] hooks, *All About Love,* xix.

[27] King, *Radical King,* 45.

[28] Ibid., 6.

[29] Baldwin, *Collected Essays,* 292.

The Church Must No Longer Be Silent about Racism in America

by Lawrence W. Rodgers

IN THIS CHAPTER, I WANT TO DISCUSS A TOPIC THAT IS VERY PER-
sonal to me. For some time, I have been wondering what kind of person
could go into a church and kill people. What kind of person can be accepted
into a place of love, peace, and acceptance, sit among them and to be
accepted into their bosom for an hour, but once that person is accepted
into this bosom of love, he or she pulls out a gun and shoots nine people:
mothers, daughters, grandmothers, fathers, sons, and grandfathers? And
for no other reason except for the fact of the color of their skin is black.

This has bothered me so much that, at the time, I stayed up all night
for several nights often in tears thinking about the poor churchgoers who
were shot down at the Emmanuel AME Church. It seemed to bother me
more than it did others that I know. I think that is because I don't see what
happened as far away or distant from me in the human experience. In fact,
when I look at my church family, I see my brothers and sisters, I see our
mothers and fathers, I see daughters and sons, and it doesn't matter what

skin pigment they have, they are my family. I love my church family! I can't imagine the horror of someone coming among my family and doing such evil.

I think the church is partially responsible for what happened in Charleston because of our silence on the issue of racial hatred. A minister-colleague once confessed to me that he knew he had members of the KKK in his church. I asked him, "How can a member of the Klan feel comfortable at your church?" If the gospel is truly preached, the gospel of love, the gospel of truth, the gospel of liberation, the gospel of repentance, the gospel of reconciliation, then hate can't exist in such an environment. Hate must leave. I don't think a member of the Klan could feel comfortable at my church because of our witness. My minister friend said in response to my question that he is afraid to preach against racial hatred because he is afraid he would lose his job. Like me, he has heard about many other ministers who were fired from their jobs when they brought diversity to their congregation or taught against racial hatred. So, the love of money and the vice of vainglory keep my friend and other ministers silent on the issue of racial hatred.

I sat back and asked myself, "What if a preacher told the shooter who killed our brothers and sisters in the church in Charleston that we are all a part of the human family?" When I look out upon the congregation where I preach, I see all shades of colors, and I view them all as my brothers and sisters.

The United States has had a problem with racism since its inception. I wonder about the Declaration of Independence, which says, "All men are created equal." I think how beautiful it is to say, "All men are created equal," but then I think about how this saying leaves out women. Also, interesting is the fact that when this phrase was penned in 1776, black men and women were enslaved in the United States. I think about why they were enslaved. It was to make money. It was to hoard resources. Oftentimes, if not all the time, when you get to the core of racial hatred what fuels it is a struggle over the resources. Even the shooter in Charleston said that he acted as he did because, "blacks are taking over the world." Clearly, this young man was confused by hate, but underneath his extreme racial hatred was a growing fear that his race was losing in the battle for resources.

This concept can be seen in the Bible in Acts 6:1–11. In this passage, the Greeks and the Hebrews were having a dispute. Actually, it was the Greek women who were having a dispute with the Hebrew women. Over what? Resources. The Greek women were not receiving the resources they required for daily life; they were being overlooked while the Hebrew women were getting what they needed. In Acts 6:1–11, we see the church appoint servants, and one of their first duties is to resolve this dispute with all of its socio-economic and ethnic tensions. They are to ensure that resources are evenly distributed.

The church leaders were able to pick up on this problem, on this tension, because they were listening to all the people. Sometimes, the talk about racism makes some feel uncomfortable, so many do not want to talk about it. Many do not want to hear about it, so it is swept under the rug where it is allowed to fester. But the church must start having this conversation.

Understanding racism is important not only from the framework of prejudice but also from its ability to limit another person's social mobility. Technically defined, a racist is a person whose prejudice and privilege combine together in a such a way so that they limit other individual's social mobility. Often racism and prejudice are confused, but the difference between the two is important to understand, especially if you are going to understand the difference between individual and systemic racism.

Individual racism is like when I was a child and was called the N-word and brutally beaten up by a group of white boys who were twice my age for not jumping over a fence to get the ball that they had kicked over it.

Systemic racism is racism in policy and public decisions. For example, from 1934 to 1968, the government backed $120 billion in home loans but refused to give home loans to black Americans for decades.[1] This practice helped create the ghettos we see today across America. It maintained segregation, it kept people from being able to invest in the future of black neighborhoods, and it made it difficult for black Americans to pass down property and wealth to their children. Keep in mind that a community with higher property taxes means better schools and better schools means better neighborhoods.

Another example is the privatized prison system essentially criminalizes black people for the purpose of re-enslaving them.[2] The 13th Amendment reads, "Neither slavery nor involuntary servitude, except as a punishment for crime whereof the party shall have been duly convicted, shall exist within the United States, or any place subject to their jurisdiction." So shortly after the Civil War ended, companies—and this still exists today—started encouraging the police to arrest blacks for frivolous reasons such as, walking on the wrong side of the street, standing or sitting idly, having too much money, having too little money, etcetera. They were arrested and thrown in work camps as free labor. Shortly after the Civil Rights movement, and many believe as a backlash to it, privatized prisons started, which use imprisoned people to work for corporate interest. People are put in these prisons using legislative practices resulting in unfair sentencing and racial profiling, resulting in the phenomenon of mass incarceration.

All these things breed tough neighborhoods with hardship, oppression, and challenges like limited resources and opportunities, and this causes hopelessness and crime. It causes one's personhood to come under attack, and you end up with awful stories like that of 16-year-old Arnesha Bowers in Baltimore who was raped and burned, allegedly as a gang initiation. The individuals who did this were wrong! Acts like this are disgusting, evil, and demonic. What happened to young Arnesha should not happen to anyone.

But when I read stories like this, I wonder how the system failed Arnesha Bowers. I wonder if her community had not been victim to systemic oppression, if her community had better jobs, if her community had more mentors, if her community had a better education system, and a better justice system, whether these boys would have been more interested in going to college than getting initiated into a gang. The church must be willing to speak out against the "internal" violence that plagues communities of all colors and backgrounds, even though it was external violence that created the internal violence.

It is difficult to free oppressed people when the oppressor gains wealth through the oppression. Look at Acts 16:16–24.

As we were going to the place of prayer, we were met by a slave
girl who had a spirit of divination and brought her owners much
gain by fortune-telling. She followed Paul and us, crying out,
"These men are servants of the Most High God, who proclaim to
you the way of salvation." And this she kept doing for many days.
Paul, having become greatly annoyed, turned and said to the
spirit, "I command you in the name of Jesus Christ to come out
of her." And it came out that very hour.

But when her owners saw that their hope of gain was gone,
they seized Paul and Silas and dragged them into the market-
place before the rulers. And when they had brought them to the
magistrates, they said, "These men are Jews, and they are disturbing our city. They advocate customs that are not lawful for
us as Romans to accept or practice." The crowd joined in attacking them, and the magistrates tore the garments off them and
gave orders to beat them with rods. And when they had inflicted
many blows upon them, they threw them into prison, ordering
the jailer to keep them safely. Having received this order, he put
them into the inner prison and fastened their feet in the stocks.

Consider what happened to Paul and Silas when they freed this slave girl.
They were beaten with rods and thrown into the worst part of the prison.
Many preachers and church leaders I know are aware of the problems I
briefly discussed in this chapter and others I haven't discussed. Yet they
refuse to speak out, to preach the gospel of Christ that liberates people
because they are afraid they will be beaten with rods, attacked, and come
under persecution. They are not willing to bear someone's cross, or even
their own cross, for the sake of liberation. Speaking frankly, although I have
spoken out about these things, I have not spoken out enough, and I realize
that I, too, have been somewhat afraid of the rods—but not anymore. I can
no longer be afraid of the rods for two reasons.

The first reason is because of what the Bible says in Revelation 21:8,
"But as for the cowardly, the faithless, the detestable, as for murderers, the

sexually immoral, sorcerers, idolaters, and all liars, their portion will be in the lake that burns with fire and sulfur, which is the second death."

I cannot be a coward. Cowards are cast into the lake of fire. Everyone faces fear, everyone gets scared, but being cowardly is when you allow fear to stop you. The church in America must not be cowardly as it deals with racism, but it must be courageous to rid the Christian community of this evil.

The second reason is, like Abraham and the patriarchs and matriarchs of the Bible, I want to leave my daughter with a better world than I lived in. I want to use my gifts and my talents, not bury them in the sand (Matt. 25:18). Rather, I want to use my talents and gifts in order to make the world she inherits a better place. I believe this is a human responsibility if we are to be God's stewards of the earth, the home God left us. We must care about the world we hand down to our children.

Romans 12:15 says, "Mourn with those who mourn." Can we mourn together? Can you sit down and mourn with me before you judge me? Oftentimes, when we see a person mourning, we say "Just get over it." We say, "Just move on," often failing to realize that the individual is still suffering from the afflictions that caused them to mourn.

When a person is abused, some individuals are quick to tell them to forgive. Yet that same individual is afraid to tell the abuser to repent. We must do both! If you have the audacity to tell an afflicted person who has a natural right to avenge himself or herself to forgive and take the godly road, you must also have the courage to tell the abuser that they are wrong, they are doing evil, they need to stop, they need to repent, they need to change. And, if possible, the repentance should come first. If it does, the abused is under an obligation to God to forgive, and this is how we have real reconciliation.

Repentance is not always about saying, "I repent." Repentance is also about giving back with interest what has been stolen, deprived, and hoarded. If you don't believe me, just ask Zacchaeus. He understood repentance well enough to know it must go beyond just words but real recompense must be substantive and not just rhetorical. This is where the church in the United States is failing in the conversation about racial reconciliation. Too many churches and religious institutions are only repenting with their tongues but their hearts, resources, and wallets are far from repentance.

Throughout history, too many in the church got it wrong. Too many in the church got it wrong on the slavery issue. Too many in the church got it wrong on segregation. Too many in the church got it wrong on racism, got it wrong on sexism, and got it wrong on many other issues.

It's time for the church to get it right. It's time for the church to be courageous. It is time for the church to wake up.

Just like when Elijah stood in front of those dry bones and asked, "Can these dry bones live?" I see the church today and I ask, Can these dry bones live? Can the church really study what Jesus was saying about being a beloved community? Can we take Jesus seriously?

Can the church get real about the problems that plague our hearts and that plague our society? Can the church push back against the evil components of our culture? Can these dry bones live and be a voice of God's will, God's love, God's grace, and God's justice?

I know that, if the church could be a real witness for Jesus in the twenty-first century, we could stop another Dylan Roof from being full of so much hate, misunderstanding, and ignorance that he goes into a church and kills innocent grandmothers, grandfathers, brothers, and sisters. It is time for the church to do better.

Discussion Questions:

1. How have you been complicit in prolonging racism?

2. How has racism and the systemic racism benefited you in life?

3. Would a member of a hate group feel welcome at your church?

4. Read Luke 19:1–10. In what ways do you need to have a Zacchaeus moment?

5. There are several organizations who engage in work to dismantle institutional racism. Visit the following organizations and discuss how their antiracist resources might be of benefit to you and your congregation:

> Southern Poverty Law Center (www.splcenter.org)
>
> Undoing Racism: The People's Institute for Survival and Beyond (www.pisab.org)
>
> Sojourners (www.sojo.net)

6. In what ways could you use antiracist strategies to help your congregation engage in antiracist work?

Notes

[1] For further information on this topic, see Alexis C. Madrigal, "The Racist Housing Policy That Made Your Neighborhood," *The Atlantic* May 22, 2014, accessed March 23, 2016, http://www.theatlantic.com/business/archive/2014/05/the-racist-housing-policy-that-made-your-neighborhood/371439/.

[2] For further information on this topic, see Michelle Alexander, *The New Jim Crow: Mass Incarceration in the Age of Colorblindness* (New York: New Press, 2010).

Well Water

John 4:1–15

by Jerry Taylor

THE GREATEST RISK TO NATIONAL SECURITY IN AMERICA TODAY IS the growing escalation of hostility along racial lines. The "us versus them" mentality among various racial groups in the United States exposes the nation's weakest vulnerability to its foreign and domestic enemies. It is common knowledge that the country's greatest weakness is racism. An enemy's probable war tactic is to divide and conquer the United States by exploiting America's unrelenting practice of racial bigotry. The exploitation of America's race problem could cause a major social disruption and could lead to a national catastrophic implosion of the country from within.

On December 29, 2008 a very disturbing article appeared in the Wall Street Journal with the title, "As if Things Weren't Bad Enough, Russian Professor Predicts End of US." At the time the article appeared, Russian academic Igor Panarin was a former KGB analyst and the dean of the Russian Foreign Ministry's Academy for Future Diplomats. He regularly appeared in the Russian media as an expert on US-Russian relations.

Professor Panarin predicted that mass immigration, the collapse of the American dollar, an economic and moral collapse would trigger a civil war and the eventual collapse and breakup of the United States. He predicted that when the going got tough the wealthier states would withhold funds from the federal government and effectively secede from the union. He said that once the United States split along ethnic lines foreign powers would move in to divide up the spoils.[1]

Since the 2008 presidential election the rise of gun sales and the increasing number of hate groups may serve as indicators that the United States could be trending in the direction of the Russian professor's predictions.

According to the Federal Bureau of Investigations (FBI), the number of Americans purchasing guns has skyrocketed since Barack Obama was elected president.[2] There has been a steady increase in background checks for gun purchase every year since 2008. Gun sale background checks for the month of January 2013 alone were 2,483,230. This totals 65,376,373 background checks completed since President Obama's first full month in office, or 44,748 background checks per day! By comparison, the number of background checks in President Obama's first term is 91.1% higher than George W. Bush's first-term total of 34,214,066. While background checks cannot be directly correlated to gun sales, it is clear that more US citizens are interested in purchasing guns than ever before. It seems as if the nation is domestically on a war footing. Talk show host Glen Beck sounds similar to the Russian professor. Mr. Beck warns that America will see riots, chaos, and assassinations in 2016. He predicts that 2016 will be a modern day 1968.

My question today is this: "Do Christians still have the moral authority to call for peace in a nation that seems to be heading towards a massive display of violent bloodletting in our streets? Can the church speak into the escalating chaos and convert the hearts and minds of our fellow Christian citizens to a pro-life stance and away from an expanding mentality that is pro-death and pro-killing? Those who rightly seek the protection of life that is in the womb must also seek to respect and protect the lives of individuals that are already here.

Our fellow citizens might point out that in the churches we have more members signing up for concealed handguns classes than we have signing up for classes on the Sermon on the Mount. How can God's children that claim to be "pro-life" engage in the massive acquisition of guns as if they are preparing to engage in violence that is "anti-life?" How can God's children who are to be called peacemakers counsel the nation to walk in the way of peace when God's children are among the voices crying for the execution of war and violence against the country's enemies?

How can Christians lead the world on the moral issue of racial unity when the church itself is divided along racial and ethnic lines? How can Christians be the salt and the light in a society that seems to be locked into what Erich Fromm[3] calls the "Syndrome of Decay,"[4] which posits that those who are psychologically disturbed lack the ability to love or to establish meaningful relationships, when Christians blatantly and unashamedly practice racial and religious apartheid? Christians will be accused of hypocrisy as long as our high sounding rhetoric about love and diversity is perfectly contradicted by the visible racial bias that exists in our churches and Christian universities. The Stone-Campbell churches in America with their emphasis on "restoration" should lead in the process of "restoring" civility among Christians within the religious community.

It was disturbing to hear a Washington official tell me that it might be close to impossible to get "Christian" Republicans and "Christian" Democrats together to discuss the racial divide from a "Christian" perspective in this country. The church's prominent and well respected ministers should be commissioned to hold politicians that claim to be Christians accountable to a higher standard in regards to racial unity.

It is a major default in the positive use of influence when we allow the sons and daughters of the church to use their affiliation with Christianity to gain political office, and the church does not encourage them to practice Christian principles within their political relationships that will lead to peace. The church should not send the sons and daughters of the church to Washington to beat the drums of war but they should be sent to serve as what Dr. Martin Luther King Jr. described as drum majors for peace.[5]

If there are any "Christian" politicians in Washington that are capable of seeking unity among believers on both sides of the political aisle it should be the sons and daughters of the Stone-Campbell churches. The Stone-Campbell churches have rightly called believers within the religious community to join the effort of "restoring" the New Testament pattern of worship and church government. The Stone-Campbell Movement's emphasis on Christian unity has in some unpronounced way found some agreement with the message of unity that drives the broader religious movement known as ecumenism.

The restoration churches have assertively fought for an authentic visible display of religious unity among believers through a literal conformity to the practice of worship found in the New Testament. Now, they should seek for an authentic visible display of spiritual unity among Christian politicians in Washington DC through a literal conformity to the practice of the doctrine of love found in the New Testament. High ranking Christian politicians in Washington DC that are affiliated with the Stone-Campbell churches should be adequately prepared in spiritual wisdom to transform a city that has become known as a city of great darkness into one that is known as a city of great light.

Stone-Campbell churches have made great progress in restoring what they believe to have been the New Testament outward practice of public worship. However, they must go further in seeking a genuine restoration of the connection of believers to the unifying essence of the Holy Spirit as defined in the New Testament. Restoration churches have not carried the restoration principle far enough if they only restore the first century practice of worship and fail to restore or reconnect twenty-first century believers to the life and power of the Holy Spirit that acted with clear definition in the first century. Churches that restore a religious form without restoring a connection to the Spirit that stands behind those forms will produce Christian politicians that go to Washington with no real spiritual power that can confront the influential political power structures that seem to over-whelm people with darkness who initially go there with good intentions.

It is imperative that we remind ourselves that the church is the body of Christ and the Holy Spirit is the Spirit of Christ. We need the physical man-ifestation of Jesus' body as well as the spiritual presence of his Holy Spirit.

Jesus and the Holy Spirit are the true change agents that can empower Christians to work in bringing about unity between different races and ethnic backgounds in this country.

Jesus demonstrates the power to change a person's attitude regarding race as he interacted with a Samaritan woman who was outside his racial and religious tribe (John 4:1–15). By doing so, Jesus violated the Jewish purity code that required Jews to remain among their own kind. Jesus displayed the courage to disregard the law of Jewish segregation and began to talk to a person that his racial/religious group considered ethnically impure and unclean.

Jesus not only associated with an unclean Samaritan, but he even went further as he asked for a drink of water from an unclean and impure Samaritan well. Not only were Jews not expected to associate with Samaritans, they weren't even supposed to eat or drink behind them. Jews simply didn't drink behind Samaritans.

Jesus said to the Samaritan woman, "Will you give me a drink?" The Samaritan woman replied, "You are a Jew, and I am a Samaritan woman. How can you ask me for a drink?" (For Jews do not associate with Samaritans.) This sounds so much like the political stalemate in Washington among "Christian" politicians in both political parties. It also sounds like what has been described as the most segregated hour in America, which is the hour of worship in many black and white churches across the United States.

The Samaritan woman was limited in her response to Jesus' request due to racial apartheid restrictions that prevented her from sharing water with a Jew. Her self-limiting belief about the separatist social roles would not permit her to respond to Jesus' thirst.

The Samaritan woman knew that Jews hated Samaritans with such intense hostility that some Jews did not even want to travel in the territory of the Samaritans, let alone share drinking water with them.

In the text, it is interesting to see that Jesus used this incident involving water to break down racial and religious barriers. The Jews had problems with the Samaritans both religiously and racially. Samaritans were viewed as being the biological result of race mixing with non-Jewish peoples. They were considered half-bred Jews. Their biologically mixed blood revealed to the Jews that the ancestors of the Samaritans had violated God's law of religious segregation. They had gone outside the Jewish people and intermingled with those who were not of God's chosen and elite race. Therefore, their theological sin revealed itself in their bloodline.

Religion and race are interconnected among Christians today. In fact, it could be successfully argued that for many "Christians" their race is their religion. This may explain why Christianity in America seems to be the last stronghold that serves as comfortable haven for those who worship the idol god of race. At the water well, Jesus challenges racial boundaries that were historically protected under the guise of the practice of "pure" religion. Jesus' action communicated his willingness to recognize the humanity of the Samaritan people in spite of the religious purity politics of his day.

As a Jew, Jesus continued to practice the religious politics of inclusion in his teachings by intentionally portraying Samaritans to Jews as heroes. Such reversal of character roles in his teachings today would get Jesus accused of practicing reverse racism. What Jesus did in his connection with the Samaritan woman at the well can be considered as taking a real "water break!" It was a "water break" in that he used the incident involving "water" to "break" down racial and religious barriers. Followers of Jesus must emulate this example today if the world is to experience the break down of racial and religious walls.

We have a water problem in America. We have a water problem in the church. There are thirsty and dehydrated people all around us. They are like the description given to Jesus in our text: tired and depleted of strength. Although as Christians we see the depleted and dehydrated condition of our fellow citizens, far too often our racial codes, religious traditions, and political loyalties won't allow us to respond compassionately to their legitimate thirst. They are the people who are just outside of our racial categories for which we feel we have no obligation to assist.

In the current narcissistic culture in the United States, not only has every individual seemed to have turned to her own way, it also seems as if every ethnic/racial group has turned inward to focus only on the needs of its members. As a nation, it seems as if we have lost the capacity to extend care and compassion to any people beyond our own racial and political categorizations. The only way Jesus would ever get water in the United States today is that he has to be "one of us."

Christians must remember that Jesus comes to us "thirsty" in all colors and races. If we ignore his thirst on the basis his skin color, his theology, or his politics, we will face a very painful and pertinent question on the last day. At that time, he will say, "When you saw me thirsty, did you give me water to drink?" At that moment, we will have to admit that we missed seeing him because he did not look like us racially, religiously, culturally, educationally, economically, and politically. We will be surprised to know that Jesus came to us thirsty in the earthen form of being black, white, hispanic, asian, Jew, gentile, democrat, and republican. Our fixation of our hatred on "them" prevented us from seeing "him" in "them!"

When we deny addressing the thirst of people on the bases of their race, we are guilty of doing what the Samaritan woman did to Jesus. She "prejudged" Jesus' attitude about her simply because she recognized him as a Jew. The woman's fixation upon a racial and religious stereotype led her to draw a false conclusion about a Jew that was like no other Jew she had met. Jesus was a Jew that was unfettered by an exclusive and racist form of religion that looked down upon outsiders as animals or subhuman at best. Jesus was a Jew that was willing to drink behind Samaritans from their own well.

The best way for Christians to start addressing America's water problem is to start taking "water breaks" together. It is time for Christians to start sharing water across racial lines. Christians of all races need to start drinking water from the same water supply.

When we are all drinking from the same water supply we will have a vested interest in making sure that the water supply remains free of the lead poisons of racism, fear of demographic changes, political discrimination, economic exploitation, and religious bigotry.

Although there are no longer water fountains with visible signs that say, "Colored Water Fountains" and "White Water Fountains," Christians continue to spiritually drink water from separate water fountains. We are still drinking from segregated wells. Racially, we cannot "get well" as long as we keep drinking polluted waters from segregated wells.

Since Christians have been born again of "water" and of the "Spirit" we should be transformed enough to show the world how different races in Christ are "getting well" by drinking the waters of eternal life from the same spiritual water well. Spiritual transformation means that we are no longer attached to the color of decaying and rotting flesh. Decaying and rotting flesh finds its refreshment by drinking water from the segregated well of racism. People that drink from the decadent waters of color seem to love the color of their skin (and kin) more than they love the colorless Spirit of Christ that dwells within.

This point reminds me of a story I grew up hearing about as a child growing up in a small black church in West Tennessee. I remember hearing some of the older family and church members talking about a white Stone-Campbell church in West Tennessee that allowed our small black congregation to use their baptistry to baptize some black converts. It was reported that after the blacks had been baptized in the baptistery, the white "Christians" drained all the water from the baptistry and scrubbed it down with Purex, Lysol, and Clorox before putting future white converts into the baptistry. I remember thinking to myself about the blood of Jesus being strong enough to clean and purify both black and white sinners alike. His blood did not need the assistance of additional cleaning agents. I would soon grow to understand that the problem was not in the water in the baptistry, but the problem was that the people were still drinking water from a polluted well filled with the waters of racism.

Jesus with the woman at the well reminds me of another incident that reveals America's "drinking" problem. I remember being the only black person at a communion service with a small, all white community of believers. There were about ten of us that sat beside each other in a half circle. I came into the service after everyone had already taken a seat. I figured I was in for an interesting experience when everyone looked shocked and surprised as if they had seen a black ghost that had just walked in. There was an open seat beside an elderly white lady. I sat down to the right of her. This meant she would be receiving communion after me. The problem was that this group drank from the same cup to share the blood of the Lord. I noticed that as the one-cup grew closer to me, the woman started to cough lightly. By the time the cup got to the person right next to me, the little lady had gone into a full blown chronic coughing episode. It was such a violent episode that it caused her to get up and walk out right as the cup got to me.

I wondered to myself whether or not the lady's coughing spell had more to do with the racial conditioning she had received than it had to do with a bad cough. I wondered whether she had been conditioned all her life not to drink behind blacks. That might have been the furthest thought from her mind, but I still questioned the real germ of her cough.

Another experience that serves as an example that the United States is still drinking from segregated wells happened when my family and I were moving from Greensboro, North Carolina to Atlanta, Georgia in 2000. Our real estate agent advised us to take all of our pictures down so that potential white buyers would not know that a black family was selling the home. The real estate agent informed us that experience proved that white buyers didn't like living behind black sellers.

In order for us to drink from a common water well, we must begin first to drink from that common "inner well" that springs up from the spiritual waters of life "within." When we are ignorant of our common "inner well," we focus more on the outer wells that keep us divided along the lines of race. I will say it again. Christians today need to engage in a "water break!" We need to break free from the segregated wells that keep filling us with the waters of hatred and hostility. Only the water of life springing up within us can empower us to break free from the polluted wells that produce the contaminated waters of racism and racial division. When we turn to the "well within," we become our own "wellness center" that can produce racial healing within us and among us.

Christians are drinking from the world's well. When we drink from the world's well, we will think like the world, hate like the world, politic like the world, dominate like the world, and kill like the world. Paul reminds us that the cup we share is a cup that is not of this fallen world. The cup that Christians share is a cup that is under the control of the Holy Spirit. Drinking from the cup of the Holy Spirit gives us a healthy attitude toward those who are racially different. However, when we stop drinking water from the world's well we will experience peer pressure from those close to us. They will wonder why we are carrying on the inherited hatred that has been passed down to us from previous generations. They will not be able to comprehend our practice of genuine racial unity.

Pressure from the world we have abandoned sometimes makes us relapse into our worldly racial attitudes. We don't like the outcast status. We don't like to be lonely or stand out. This is why Paul rebuked Peter in Galatians 2:11–21. Peter practiced hypocrisy in that he fellowshipped with the Gentiles until the Jews from Antioch showed up. When his group arrived, he distanced himself fearing what the Jews would say about his open fellowship with uncircumcised Gentiles. He could not stand the thought of being ousted. He valued drinking from his old polluted religious/racial well above drinking water from the life giving well water of Christ. Peter was like the king in the short parable below that could not stand to be viewed as an outsider by his own people.

The King and The Poisoned Well

There was once a wise king who ruled over a vast kingdom. He was feared for his might and loved for his wisdom. Now in the heart of the city, there was a well with pure and crystalline waters from which the king and all the inhabitants drank. When all were asleep, three witches entered the city and poured seven drops of a strange liquid into the well. They said that henceforth all who drink this water should become mad.

The next day, all the people drank of the water, but not the king. And the people began to say, "The king is mad and has lost his reason. Look how strangely he behaves. We cannot be ruled by a madman, so he must be dethroned."

The king grew very fearful, for his subjects were preparing to rise against him. He had a difficult choice: risk being destroyed by his beloved subjects or drink from the poisoned well and become mad like them. So that evening, he ordered a golden goblet to be filled from the well, and he drank deeply. The next day, there was great rejoicing among the people, for their beloved king had finally regained his reason.

As we listen to many voices in our nation today there seems to be a great deal of madness. Evidence is everywhere that someone has poisoned the city well in the United States. Those who refuse to drink from the city well are attacked because they choose to act and speak reasonably and civilly. Those who don't engage in demonstrating madness are defined as being weak. The mad people are not able to understand why more people are not "mad!" The only way that Christians can escape from the madness is that we must learn to drink from the inner well that Jesus said would spring up with eternal waters of life. We must learn to dwell in that well.

Despite all the negativity we see going on around us in the name of political discourse, we must be determined to dwell in the well. You will be persecuted because you don't run with the mad crowd, but dwell in your well. Family members will reject you and write you out of the family will, but dwell in your well. You will be called a traitor to your race and maybe even be accused of treason, but dwell in your well. As you dwell in your well, when others ask you how you are doing under intense pressure and persecution, you will be able to say to them that it is well with your soul.

Discussion Questions

1. Discuss ways in which you have a "water problem."

2. Do we have an obligation to engage the political process? In what ways can we hold elected politicians accountable to a higher standard in regards to racial reconciliation? What would that look like?

3. The author encourages us to "start sharing water across racial lines". What does that look like?

Notes

[1] Andrew Osborn, "As if Things Weren't Bad Enough, Russian Professor Predicts End of U.S." *Wall Street Journal* 252,152 (Dec 29, 2008): pA1-A7. 2p.

[2] Federal Bureau of Investigations, "NICS Firearm Background Checks: Month/Year," (November 30, 1998-February 29, 2016) Reports and Statistics, accessed March 22, 2016, https://www.fbi.gov/about-us/cjis/nics/reports/nics_firearm_checks_-_month_year.pdf.

[3] Erich Fromm (1900–1980), a German social psychologist associated with the Frankfurt School of Critical Theory.

[4] Erich Fromm, *The Heart of Man: It's Genius for Good and Evil* (New York: Harper & Row, 1964).

[5] Martin Luther King, Jr., "The Drum Major Instinct," in *A Knock at Midnight: Inspiration from the Great Sermons of Reverand Martin Luther King, Jr.*, eds. Carson and Holloran (New York: Warner Books, 1998), 165–86.

Concrete
Examples

Seeking Higher Ground

Bringing to Light Microaggressions That Impede Progress
on the Road to the Beloved Community

by William Lofton Turner

THE YEAR 2014 MARKED THE FIFTIETH ANNIVERSARY OF THE PAS-
sage of the Civil Rights Act, a landmark piece of legislation in the United
States that outlawed discrimination based on race, color, religion, sex, or
national origin. It ended the legally sanctioned, unequal application of
voter registration requirements and racial segregation in schools, at the
workplace, and by facilities that served the general public. Although the
impact of this historic law has been rather far-reaching and generally constructive and beneficial with respect to bringing forth racial integration in
American society, even among those institutions beyond its explicit power
and purview, one area where its impact and influence has been noticeably
lacking has been in our faith communities. Today, our churches are among
the most racially segregated organizations in American society.[1] This reality
is especially true among Churches of Christ. Although there are examples

of a few congregations that have racially and ethnically diverse member-
ships and regular attendants, the vast majority are overwhelming racially
segregated.

It is clear that the church, as recounted in the Book of Acts, was multicultural, and like a tapestry, made up of many strands of thread, the
church was woven together to create a beautiful cloth. As in a tapestry,
each thread is like each person and groups of similar threads symbolically
represents each of the various cultures that come together. Although the
types of threads differ in many ways—some can be thick, thin, coarse, or
smooth—the various threads, when woven together, achieve a beautiful
image. The tapestry metaphor beautifully conveys how the individual-
ity of every person and culture can come together in a harmonious and
unexpected way. A spool of only one type of thread could not be woven
into any type of image. Both variation and interaction are needed to create
something truly beautiful. The church, like a tapestry, is most brilliant when
all of the elements of its construction are working together. Why then are
we so separate? Why are the practices of engagement and interaction the
exception rather than the rule? Why have secular communities outpaced
faith communities in unifying and increasing interactions among its constituents? Well it appears that there may be some defects in the tapestry.

Our Shared Tapestry

Dr. Martin Luther King shared with his supporters at the end of the
Montgomery bus boycott in 1956, "the end is reconciliation, the end is
redemption, the end is the creation of the beloved community."[2] With these
words, he declared that their common goal was not simply the end of segregation as an institution. Rather, King popularized a new vision of a "beloved
community" that reflected the strong religious convictions that motivated
the civil rights movement in the South in its early days. Standing courageously on the Judeo-Christian foundations of their moral commitments,
civil rights leaders sought to transform the social and political realities of
twentieth-century America. In many ways there has been progress, though
there is much left to be done. Why, though, has this spiritual vision and
enlightenment so eluded the uniting of our churches along racial lines?

Perhaps we have not exerted the moral vigor and determination needed to bring about change. However, the same spiritual vision that animated the civil rights movement remains at our disposal today, as a vital source of moral energy. I believe that we are in need of a new exuberance of an old vision for Christianity that will allow us to reclaim and demonstrate the centrality of faith in the quest for social justice and authentic community. In order to do this, we must come to grips with the inconvenient truths of our pasts. History is important and offers lessons for our path forward including lessons learned from the mistakes we have made.

We cannot move forward while we are still living with an unresolved and unrepentant past. As a nation, we have not lived up to our calling with respect to creating a racially harmonious community. Although we have begun to address the legal concerns by removing many of the legislative barriers that separate us and by creating other laws that encourage interaction, their impact on personal decision-making have been limited. As a church community, our efforts toward reconciliation have been less than robust. Our racial circumstance brings to mind the Israelites prayer of reconciliation recorded in the Book of Nehemiah, in which their efforts to rebuild the holy city and begin anew started with an acknowledgement and confession of their past failures and mistakes as well as developing an understanding of what it would take to repair, reconcile, and move forward (Nehemiah 9:5–36). I contend that we are at this point relative to racial reconciliation. So, what is delaying our progress?

In 1963, Dr. King penned his now famous "Letter from the Birmingham Jail," while he was imprisoned for civil disobedience. Here, he outlined the method and reasoning for non-violent direct action to end segregation. The Letter is a response to a public letter of concern and caution that King had received from eight white southern clergy. They had cautioned King to pause, and even though progress was extremely slow-moving, to give more time for the systems of the day to respond and to wait for a more "convenient season." Recognizing that these advisors were lacking in their understanding of the urgency and seriousness of the matter, King replied: "Shallow understanding from people of good will is more frustrating than absolute misunderstanding from people of ill will. Lukewarm acceptance is much more bewildering than outright rejection."[3]

This essay focuses on the impact of lukewarm acceptance and the difficulties of shallow understanding from people of goodwill, which is far more subtle and insidious than blatant racism and outright bigotry. As I embark upon this conversation, I begin with the true belief, that many, if not most of the readers of this treatise are people of goodwill. I, too, believe myself to be a person of good will. I believe that we all want to be better, to solve this racially divisive predicament, and to move forward with a more productive approach. So what I am prodding in this essay is an honest conversation on race for people of goodwill. However, as Dr. King offered in his now famous "Letter from a Birmingham Jail," being a person of goodwill is important but not sufficient. Timely and intentional actions are required.[4]

I also assume that most of us aspire to be a church of acceptance and plurality. As a faith tradition, I trust that many in Churches of Christ recognize the failures of our collective pasts regarding diversity and inclusivity and acknowledge that we are at a precipice with respect to understanding and valuing the Biblical imperative and example of embracing multiculturalism. We are learning the value of honoring our differences, for that is where the richness of interaction and engagement reside. We also know that welcoming and embracing our diversity can often be complicated. Misunderstandings can occur and often do occur. Our differing opinions, expressions, and experiences often prompt collisions and discomfort. Many of our conflicts will be about power, at times explicit, but most often covert and coercive. We should anticipate such occurrences. However, our willingness to work through the awkwardness of racial and cultural immersion will save the day.

The notion of the beloved community envisioned by King is a society based on justice, equal opportunity, and love of one's fellow human beings.[5] The Beloved Community closely resembles the church in that both are based on value systems that reflect the teachings of Jesus Christ. Like the church, the beloved community is not a perfect paradise. Though made up of differing and often intersecting parts, woven tightly like the nap of a tapestry, there are tears and picks in the tapestry requiring attention and repair most of the time.

I refer to the tears and rips in the tapestry as microaggressions. What are microaggressions? They are "brief and commonplace verbal, behavioral, or environmental indignities, whether intentional or unintentional, that communicate hostile, derogatory, or negative racial slights and insults toward people of color."[6] This term, coined in the 1970s by psychiatrist Chester Pierce, reemerged in literature of psychology and other social sciences largely due to the award-winning work of Columbia University professor of psychology, Derald Wing Sue. Subsequently, it became a part of the popular lexicon of American culture a little over a decade ago. Some scholars, philosophers, and other deep thinkers have embraced it as a brilliant concept and explanation of the observed human behaviors and experiences associated with the coercion and oppression of marginalized and subjugated groups while others have critiqued and rejected it as meaningless psychobabble and politically correct drivel. However, there is ample scientific evidence supporting its validity and because of the weightiness of the supporting scientific evidence and its growing acceptance by social scientists of varying disciplines, I am compelled to place it under a magnifying glass for closer inspection to determine its relevance to the churches journey to reconciliation and the Christian journey to create a beloved community.

Microaggressions: A Deeper Gaze

Sue and his colleagues identify three types of microaggressions.

1. A microinsult is characterized by communications that convey rudeness and insensitivity and demean a person's racial heritage or identity (for example, eye rolling and dismissiveness during a discussion about an individual's racial identity).
2. Microinvalidations are communications that exclude, negate, or nullify the psychological thoughts, feelings, or experiential reality of a person of color. Examples of microinvalidation could be multiplied, but two will suffice:

- A white person stating to a person of color that they "don't see color," denying the existence of racial and ethnic experiences.
- An individual who considers racial or cultural perspectives to be childish or reflective of a character flaw. The argument, "If you would just toughen up and not be so sensitive, your problems would be greatly reduced" always invalidates and belittles.

3. A microassault is an explicit racial derogation characterized primarily by a verbal or nonverbal attack meant to hurt the intended victim. This can happen through name-calling, avoidant behavior, or purposeful discriminatory actions. Microassaults against African American people also appear in the form of unflattering and stereotypic depictions or the depiction of white actors/models in black face, or associations between black people and negative and aggressive behaviors that paint all members of the race with a broad brush. Microassaults are typically more conscious and deliberate than other forms of microaggression.

Microaggressive acts are sometimes clear and recognizable, but they are more often subtle and hard to define, articulate, and address. In fact, "the power of racial microaggressions lies in their invisibility to the perpetrator and, oftentimes, the recipient."[7] The burden of interpreting and responding to a microaggressive act falls on the individual. The victim must determine whether the incident was intentional or perhaps reflects misunderstanding or ignorance, and then make a decision about whether or not to address it. Bringing attention to the incident may promote a further negative response, such as anger, denial, and accusations. Microaggressive acts need not be specific or verbal but can refer to environments that are either intentionally or unintentionally unsupportive to a person because of his or her racial identity.

Microaggressions affect the psyche of the individual victim and the group of which he or she belongs. They also deliver persistent, inaccurate messages about a group of people and, as a result, obscure the true cultural nature of the group and replace it with a stereotype. While each event might be tolerated in isolation, the overall cumulative effect of microaggressions can be devastating.[8] Microaggressions are significant because research suggests that daily discrimination can result in more distress and stronger negative health outcomes than time-limited episodic discrimination.[9]

Unlike the racial slurs and insults of old, the novel offering of this work is the notion that microaggressions are often unintentional and seemingly, to the aggressor, insignificant. Generally speaking, we are talking about what might seem to some to be throw-away phrases and actions rather than overt "hate-speech" or overtly violent conduct. Unlike blatant and overt racism, micoraggressive actions are understated and indirect. Whereas macroaggressive action is like an explosion caused by a bomb, microaggressions are more akin to dripping water onto a rock that has a damaging and erosive impact over a period of time. Microaggessions are often likened to resemble death by a thousand cuts rather than a knife to the heart. Both, however, have the same ultimate harmful effects.

Microaggressions are a form of contemporary violence experienced by persons from minority groups or communities. Microaggressions are current events, and are often covert in nature. They are defined as "events involving discrimination, racism, and daily hassles that are targeted at individuals from diverse racial and ethnic groups.[10] Microaggressions are chronic and can occur on a daily basis. Microaggressions and the micro-aggresive acts can perpetuate the trauma.

Sue notes that "the most detrimental forms of microaggressions are usually delivered by well-intentioned individuals who are unaware that they have engaged in harmful conduct toward a socially devalued group."[11] These everyday occurrences may on the surface appear quite harmless, trivial, or be described as "small slights," but research indicates they have a powerful impact upon the psychological well-being of marginalized groups and affect their standard of living by creating inequities in health care, education, and employment."

Microaggressions are harmful because of the indirect and underlying messages that they communicate. Offenders are often consciously unaware of their violations because their biases are often implicit and unconsciously held. The message received by the sender often goes beyond the explicit message that the sender intended. For example, several years ago when our daughter was a toddler, my family and I were shopping in a large mall department store. Morgan, our daughter, like her mother and I, is African American. While we shopped, Morgan was approached by a well-dressed white lady probably in her 50s, whom I assumed was mesmerized by Morgan's beauty and playfulness. This was a common occurrence at that time in her life. The lady, I believe well-meaningly, engaged Morgan and commented over and over again to my daughter her delight at how beautiful and clean she was. My first thought was that this is a rather odd and awkward comment, but I dismissed it as nothing more than awkward phraseology as we walked away with Morgan. Granted, this is not the usual commendation bestowed upon a four-year old girl in a fancy department store. But the lady went on to mention her cleanliness several more times, each time more animated than the last, seemingly incredulous that this child was not hygienically challenged. I feel rather certain that her explicit message to my child was meant as a compliment. However, her underlying message to me as her parent was that of incredulity, "I don't expect African American children to be cared for and cleaned up by their parents."

This incident, in and of itself, seems rather innocuous. However, when these types of behaviors happen repeatedly, day in and day out and trigger historical memory, they have the power to impact a person's psyche and soul in negative ways. The message that I received was belittling and judgmental. It joined a long list of other "I didn't expect you to be" sentiments. I am surprised that you are ——————— ... fill in the blank—clean, smart, articulate, good, moral. Much of this behavior is rooted in the culturally insidious and pervasive fallacies related to white racial supremacy. However, these implicit biases bring about myriad abreactions and harmful consequences including: creating a sense of exclusion and marginalization, negatively impacting one's sense of belonging, negatively impacting one's level of comfort and trust in engaging with others, impeding performance in academics and interviews, hampering chances of success, diminishing one's sense of personal validation, and harmfully impacting one's overall health. When all was said and done, my four-year-old looked the lady squarely in the eyes with pure innocence and kindness said, "Thank you, I think you are clean too."

The targets of microaggressions are not just people of color. Although Sue's (2010a; Sue et al, 2007) research began with the experiences of people of color, he soon saw that this was a universal experience for anyone of a minority identity: women, religious minorities, people with disabilities and so on. Other examples of microaggressive behavior include:

- When a female physician wearing a stethoscope is assumed to be a nurse rather than a physician. The message may not have been intentional but it is there. Women are less capable than men.
- When a female African American graduate student emerges from a Saturday of studying at the library carrying a stack of books (as PhD students are likely to do), and is stopped and searched by the campus police, when no other student was stopped or searched. The message received: You don't belong here.

Sadly, this is a true story. This young woman, a highly decorated and recruited honor student of mine at a very large and distinguished upper mid-western university was devastated, having been accosted and surrounded by several police officers and flashing police cars while being searched out in the open as her fellow graduate students watched.

As her major doctoral advisor, on Monday morning I called a meeting of the director of the campus police, the officer, and my student to ask for an explanation and to make sense of the situation.

- Had she comported herself in a manner that was inappropriate and different from other graduate students?
- Was she dressed in a fashion that seemed inappropriate for the setting and different than the norm?
- Had she been offensive in her speech or behavior that day?

The answer to all of those questions was no. The officer admitted that she was very well spoken, that she hadn't resisted their inquiries, but nonetheless was made to feel as though she had done something wrong. Had there been a report of suspicious activity or concern involving someone who resembled my student? No, there had been no such report. The police officer's only explanation was that she seemed suspicious and out of place and he was doing his job by checking his hunch. He couldn't or wouldn't offer any further explanation as to why she was singled out. The only apology offered was, "We're sorry that you felt singled out." My student never felt safe again at the University. Her spirit was forever changed. I and the other members of the faculty persuaded her to stay on and complete her doctoral degree, which she did, again with honors, but it jaded her sense of safety and security in a place that she had chosen to develop her career.

Another final example involves an African American male professor at a large elite university, an endowed chair, relatively new to the university, goes for an early evening walk across campus after a three-hour stint in the classroom and is stopped and interrogated by the campus police, in a rapid fire manner, as to the reason for his presence on campus, why he's here, where he lives and where his office is located. The professor gently and quietly said, "I have my faculty ID if you would like to see it." Upon showing the officers the ID, they simply said, "Have a nice evening."

That person was me. The whole incident left me with a sense of unease. After all, shouldn't professors be on campus? I spent the next several days mulling over the event and questioning what I might have done to cause their suspiciousness. I was dressed in typical professorial garb. I was walking at a comfortable gait and out in the open. I could not think of a reason. I spent time thinking what to do about the incident. Should I report this to the chancellor? Should I complain to the police captain? I knew I felt bad because of the incident and I did not want anyone else to feel that way. The message I received was that I did not belong and that I would always need to be guarded and mindful about my behavior in that setting, even though I did not know what I "should" have done differently.

This microaggression was powerful to me because it harkened back to macroaggressions in the culture. I thought of all of the black men who have been stopped and questioned by the police for no apparent reason or the judgments that have been made about a person's character just because of their skin color or outward appearance didn't match the approved profile of an observer.

Ironically, this incident occurred in 2009, only two months after an event at the near campus home of famed Harvard University Professor Henry Louis Gates. Given the media attention at the time, should not university police department have a heightened awareness of the damaging impact of these types of mistakes? In the course of my fifteen-minute walk, I saw dozens of professors, workers, and others who were behaving similarly to me. None of them were people of color. This incident changed my sense of belonging for the remainder of my tenure there.

Historical Trauma

It is within the human condition to experience trauma. Trauma can be defined as events, circumstances, and impacts that overwhelm an individual's, institution's, or system's capacity to integrate and process.[12] I am suggesting that the racial behaviors aimed at people of color have been traumatizing and continue to have a traumatic impact on their existence. Trauma-informed approaches to racial healing require consciously building structures, strategies and pathways, and environments that are restorative in nature, promote resilience, and acknowledge and avoid inflicting further trauma.

Historical trauma is defined as "a constellation of characteristics associated with massive cumulative group trauma across generations."[13] Historical trauma differs from other types of trauma in that the traumatic event is shared by a collective group of people who experience the consequences of the event, as well as the fact that the impact of the trauma is held personally and can be transmitted over generations. Children of survivors can experience symptoms similar to their parents despite the fact that they were not directly exposed to the trauma. Examples of historical trauma include planned violence or segregation (enslavement, genocide, massacres, imprisonment), prevention of cultural or spiritual practices (forced conversion designed to deculturate and assimilate an entire group of people), and environmental decisions (radioactive dumping in specific geographic areas that affect specific groups of people).

There have been numerous studies of the intergenerational transmission of trauma. The phenomenon was first observed in 1966 by clinicians who were alarmed by and concerned about the number of children of survivors of the Nazi Holocaust seeking treatment in Canada.[14] Some research has shown that children of Holocaust survivors may experience a stress vulnerability that is greater than their peers.[15] Children of survivors may not exhibit clinical symptoms as a result of their parent's trauma, but they may experience greater trauma when faced with a new stressor. Nagata, Trierweiler, and Talbot have extensively explored the experiences of the descendants of Japanese Americans interned in camps during World War II.[16] Findings suggest that historical trauma associated with internment may account for differences in confidence, self-esteem, assertiveness, shame, and family communication. Also, Nagata has explained how those interned at very young ages, though too young to remember many of the camp events, nevertheless carry the burden of this past and may explore its psychological significance only after entering therapy in adult life."[17] Studies of events that lead to historical trauma among communities of color have revealed three distinguishing characteristics:

- The traumatic events are widespread and many people either experienced or were affected by the events;
- The events generate high levels of collective distress and mourning in contemporary communities;
- The events are usually perpetrated by outsiders with purposeful and often destructive intent.[18]

In order for us to achieve our reconciliation, we must recognize that a reciprocal relationship exists between racial equity and trauma. In order to do racial equity work, it must be trauma-informed, and vice versa. Trauma-informed racial equity approaches transparently value healing as part of the change process, integrate the realities and effects of historical oppressions in analyses, and address racial microaggressions and implicit bias in addition to structural barriers.

Facing A Difficult Past

So how do we speak to each other's souls without blaming? First, we have to understand how we got where we currently are and then we can begin to make shifts. But why is understanding what occurred in past decades, even centuries, relevant to our plight today? Because there are issues that remain unresolved and the residual effects are alive and well and impactful today.

The United States has had a sad and very difficult history with respect to racial inequality and inequity that harkens back to the slavery era.[19] For varying reasons, this era was a painful and shaming time and its residual effects continue to be a source of discomfort. As with most uncomfortable topics, we either avoid discussions about these matters or find ways of distracting ourselves by changing the conversation to something less threatening. We fear this topic because we believe that it has the power to elicit anger, guilt, blame, and shame or opening wounds and reliving unresolved pain. We are fearful of exposing ourselves by revealing our deeply held ideas and opinions that might be out of fashion. We fear slipping up and saying something harmful in the heat of the moment that will be difficult to take back. We are fearful because we run the risk of opening ourselves to ridicule and shame. Because we have never really truly talked about these matters and their debilitating impact of people on all sides, that legacy continues to evolve. Truth and reconciliation requires facing the truth as a necessary precursor of reconciliation.

Even though we have a lot of shared remembrances around the nineteenth century, we really don't talk about the legacy of slavery and its impact on our present day thinking. We imagine that if we keep quiet, it and its ensuant problems will all go away. However, silence has the effect of keeping the wound open and obstructing healing. There were myths created about African Americans during slavery, not just that they were enslaved but that they are somehow deficient, not smart, not capable, that they needed an institution like slavery to organize them, to make them productive, and save them from themselves. Slavery also created some harmful myths about whites. One in particular was the myth of racial superiority.[20]

Myriad evils accompanied the enslavement of men and women of African descent. However, as noted by Stevenson, the great evil of American slavery was not only the involuntary servitude, nor the forced labor, or even the blatant disregard of the humanity of a whole race of human beings. The great evil of American slavery was the narrative of racial difference that was created that has outlasted many of the direct and overt behaviors that have accompanied this fabricated and ill-informed set of beliefs. In particular, the ideology of white supremacy that it fabricated: the idea that because one's skin is white, then one is superior or because one's skin is black or brown another is inferior.[21]

What brought this about? What is at the heart of this atrocious fabrication? We, as a nation, accepted and embraced this notion because slave owners wanted to feel just and moral and Christian while they owned other human beings. In order to do this, they had to see the people that they owned as less than fully human.[22]

Bryan Stevenson has noted in his elegant treatise, *Just Mercies: A Story of Justice and Redemption*, that neither the Emancipation Proclamation, which ended slavery in the states of the confederacy, nor the Thirteenth Amendment to the US Constitution, which brought to an end slavery and involuntary servitude, deal with this narrative of racial difference or the ideology of white supremacy. That is in part, why slavery did not fully end, it just evolved into decades of other devastating and trauma producing practices such as lynchings, racial terrorism, and Jim Crow, all to support and sustain the racial hierarchy propagated by the doctrine of white supremacy.

Unlike many ethnic and racial groups in the United States, African Americans are not here because of immigration but are the descendants of slaves. The very states, cities, and counties that we live in were structured because of the legacy of slavery. As recounted by Isabela Wilkinson, the whole demographic geography of the nation was shaped by the racial terror that followed slavery. Black people in Oakland, Los Angeles, Chicago, Detroit, Cleveland, New York, Philadelphia, and Washington, DC are there because of the terror that followed slavery.[23] The very counties in the southern states or parts of town in southern cities are there due to the forced segregation imposed upon them by law. These people of color fled to these communities, not as immigrants looking for new opportunities in a new country, but as traumatized refugees from lynchings, violence, imprisonment, and Jim Crow indignities.

Negative Outcomes for Those in Disempowered Groups

Studies have shown that the following common characteristics result from exposure to historical trauma, and notes their similarity in response to those identified in the Holocaust literature: anxiety, intrusive trauma imagery, depression, survivor guilt, elevated mortality rates from cardiovascular diseases as well as suicide and other forms of violent death, identification with ancestral pain and deceased ancestors, psychic numbing and poor affect tolerance, and unresolved grief.[24]

Negative Outcomes for Those in Empowered Groups

On cognitive, emotional, behavioral, and spiritual levels, psychology research indicates that when microaggressive perpetrators become increasingly aware of their biases, they often experience debilitating emotional turmoil (guilt, fear, defensiveness), cognitive distortion and constriction— false sense of reality, and behavioral avoidance or inauthentic actions that impair relationships with marginalized individuals and/or groups.[25] Much of the focus in psychology has been the discussion and analysis of racial and gender microaggressions on the recipients; especially with respect to their harmful impact upon people of color. However, increasing interest and scholarly works on the psychosocial costs of racism have spawned renewed interest in looking at the detrimental impact of microaggressions on those who oppress.

Cognitive Costs of Oppression

Scholars and humanists have argued that being an oppressor requires a dimming of perceptual awareness and accuracy that is associated with self-deception.[26] They note that few oppressors are completely unaware of their roles in the oppression and degradation of others. To continue in their oppressive ways means they must engage in denial and live a false reality that allows them to function in good conscience. Second, the oppressors' empowered status over marginalized groups may have a corrupting influence in the ability to attune to the plight of marginalized groups.[27] In essence, an imbalance of power acutely affects perceptual accuracy and diminishes reality testing. For example, in the corporate world, women must attune to the feelings and actions of their male colleagues in order to survive in a male culture. People of color must be constantly vigilant to read the minds of their oppressors lest they incur their wrath. Those in empowered groups, however, aren't required to understand the thoughts, beliefs or feelings of various marginalized groups to survive. Their actions are not accountable to those without power and they need not understand them to function effectively.[28]

Affective Costs of Oppression

When racism or sexism is pushed into the consciousness of oppressors, they are likely to experience a mix of strong and powerful disruptive emotions. These intense feelings represent emotional roadblocks to self-exploration and must be deconstructed if oppressors are to continue in their journey to self-reckoning. These feelings include the following:

1. Fear, anxiety, and apprehension are common and powerful feelings that arise when race or gender related situations present themselves. The fear may be directed at members of marginalized groups; that they are dangerous, will do harm, are prone to violence, or may contaminate the person. Thus, avoidance of certain group members and restricting interactions with them may be chosen.

2. Guilt is also another strong and powerful emotion that many whites experience when racism is brought to their awareness. As we have indicated, an attempt to escape guilt and remorse means dulling and diminishing one's own perception. Knowledge about race-based advantages, the continued mistreatment of large groups of people, the realization that people have personally been responsible for the pain and suffering of others, elicits strong feelings of guilt. Guilt creates defensiveness and outbursts of anger in an attempt to deny, diminish and avoid such a disturbing self-revelation.

3. Low empathy and sensitivity towards the oppressed is another outcome of oppression for the perpetrator. The harm, damage, and acts of cruelty visited upon marginalized groups can only continue if the person's humanity is diminished; they lose sensitivity to those that are hurt; they become hard, cold and

unfeeling to the plight of the oppressed; and they turn off their compassion and empathy for others. To continue being oblivious to one's own complicity in such acts, means objectifying and dehumanizing people being oppressed. In many respects, it means separating oneself from others, seeing them as lesser beings, and in many cases treating them like subhuman aliens.

Behavioral Costs of Oppression

Behaviorally, the psychosocial costs of racism include fearful avoidance of diverse groups and/or diversity activities and experiences in our society, impaired interpersonal relationships, pretense and inauthenticity in dealing with racial and gender topics, and acting in a callous and cold manner toward fellow human beings.[29]

Fearful avoidance deprives oppressors the richness of possible friendships and an expansion of educational experiences that open up life horizons and possibilities. If we use racism as an example, there is great loss in depriving oneself of interracial friendships, forming new alliances, and learning about differences related to diversity. Self-segregation because of fear of certain groups in our society and depriving oneself of multicultural/ diversity experiences constrict one's life possibilities and results in a narrow view of the world.

Spiritual and Moral Costs of Oppression

In essence, oppression inevitably means losing one's humanity for the power, wealth and status attained from the subjugation of others. One loses a spiritual connectedness with fellow human beings and fails to recognize the polarities of the spiritual and democratic principles of equality and the inhuman and unequal treatment of the oppressed. It means turning a blind eye to treating marginalized groups like second-class citizens, imprisoning groups on reservations, concentration camps, inferior schools, segregated neighborhoods, prisons and life-long poverty. It means justifying the harmful and negatively treatment of whole races of people or entire religious groups based on the bad actions of a few. To allow the continued degradation, harm, and cruelty to the oppressed means diminishing one's humanity, and lessening compassion toward others. People who oppress must, at some level, become callous, cold, hard, and unfeeling toward the plight of the oppressed. In the parable of the sheep and goats recorded in Matthew 25, those accused of neglecting those who were relatively disenfranchised seemed genuinely surprised by the charges levied against them. Those accused answered, "Lord, when did we see you hungry or thirsty or a stranger or needing clothes or sick or in prison, and did not help you?" (Matt. 25:40). The reply from the Lord was, "Truly I tell you, whatever you did not do for one of the least of these, you did not do for me" (Matt. 25:41).Perhaps they were in this spiritually calloused state brought on by their neglect and dehumanization of those who were different than them, persons that they deemed to be less important than themselves.

In summary, racial and gender microaggressions are manifestations of oppression. They remain invisible because of a cultural conditioning process that allows perpetrators to discriminate without knowledge of their complicity in the inequities visited upon marginalized groups. The costs of inaction for perpetrators can be calculated in the cognitive, emotional, behavioral, and spiritual toll to oppressors.

Conclusion

We as human beings hold prejudices. In the United States, we hold prejudices because we have been taught and trained and pushed to believe that those who are seemingly different than ourselves are to be feared and avoided. Over the past several decades, we, as a nation, have been corrupted by the politics of fear and anger, where we quickly judge or even demonize those we consider to be the "other," whether different by faith, or race, or culture. We have been told to fear those who impress us as the other. We've been told to be afraid. We've been told to be angry. We have separated ourselves from people who are unlike us. We literally lock people away and segregate ourselves from those who look, think, and speak differently. We are prompted to think of the world in terms of "us and them." Consequently, we don't see "them" in their totality, we don't interact with "them" in meaningful ways, and we don't worship with "them" although we proclaim the same faith. When we are distant from "them," we may feel things about "those people" that might not be complete or fair. When we don't elect to see "them," when they are distant, it might be much easier to imagine that theirs is a world that you don't need to spend any time thinking about. Clearly, this is a problem.

If ever there was a place where racial harmony, acceptance of difference and unity should exist, it is in our churches; and yet churches, including and perhaps especially Churches of Christ, are among the most racially segregated institutions in our society. This is rather puzzling and troubling reality given that the teachings and example of Jesus, whom we claim as our sovereign, were antithetical to these mindsets and behaviors. Yet, this is the current reality. Both our national and ecumenical racial histories are unsettling and often make us uncomfortable. These divergent and unsettling racial perspectives are problems that have been with us for a long period of time. Unfortunately, we have dealt with this particular set of problems by not dealing with them, through avoidance, externalizing blame, and distancing ourselves from the harsh realities associated with these concerns.

Christ opted to get close to the problems faced by humanity. Following Jesus' example, it would seem likely that we would choose to get close to problems, to go to where the problems actually are, and to use our talents and skills to solve problems. Instead, we often behave contradictorily. Consider the choices we make to separate ourselves from the problems associated with the dearth of racial harmony: we decide, residentially, to live apart from one another; we construct barriers, educationally, to learn in different spaces; and most lamentably, we rationalize reasons and create justifications for worshipping separately. When overtures are made to join together, they typically follow the historical myth of white supremacy where those from predominately black and brown congregations are invited to assimilate into the predominately white congregations under their current leadership structure and worship culture. If changes are to occur, we should actually get closer to these problems, get proximate to the problem, and deal openly and honestly with them. This isn't about merely throwing money at a situation as is often the case in these matters. Again, drawing on the wisdom of Martin Luther King:

A true revolution of values will soon cause us to question the fairness and justice of many of our past and present policies. On the one hand, we are called to play the Good Samaritan on life's roadside, but that will be only an initial act. One day we must come to see that the whole Jericho Road must be transformed so that men and women will not be constantly beaten and robbed as they make their journey on life's highway. True compassion is more than flinging a coin to a beggar. It comes to see that an edifice which produces beggars needs restructuring.[30]

As members of the beloved community, we are directed to forge ahead toward finding solutions to our human problems, to move onward toward higher ground. However, we will never truly move forward until we face our pasts. Failure to understand the problem leaves us all broken and trapped in a cycle of denial, mistrust and misunderstanding. The motive and goals for these realizations are not to blame and create guilt, but to enlighten us by fostering deeper understanding among us, to heal us by nurturing and fostering empathy for our fellow human family, and to free us from fear and guilt that binds us through our anger and shame.

As with most problems, there is a story behind our nation's and our churches' racial past. There were stories and myths woven into the tapestry of racial misunderstanding to provide justification for the ownership of other human beings and their continued degradation as a people. These were stories that were repeated again and again, that propagated untruths about the inferiority of one group and the superiority of another. These narratives have been harmful and enduring. The proliferation of these untruthful and destructive narratives has damaged all of us and continues to hinder the healing and reconciliation required for spiritual, affective and cognitive restoration and growth to occur for all in our culture. Sadly, those who proclaim Christian faith, who regularly attend church, have fared only slightly better, if at all, than nonbelievers.

An important part of the work of the church is to change these harmful and toxic narratives to narratives that are based in truth, spirituality, and virtue. Our job is to figure out how we change these narratives. Change begins with examining and lasting change comes about through action and changing narratives. Changing narratives is very hard work, but I am persuaded that if we are going to really heal, that is what we are going to need to think about as we move forward.

Discussion Questions

1. Watch the video, "I, Too, Am Harvard", a short documentary about microaggressions experienced by students on the campus of Harvard University. And, then watch "The Invisible Discriminator", an Australian anti-racism commercial. Discuss the similarities and differences in each video.[31]

2. In what ways can microaggressions impede progress towards racial reconciliation in your congregation? What steps can you take to further progress?

3. The author asks us to read Nehemiah 9:5–36 to "develop an understanding of what it would take to repair, reconcile, and move forward". After reading that scripture, identify ways in which you could individually and collectively acknowledge and confess past failures and mistakes related to microaggressions and racial reconciliation.

4. Research the history of your congregation. What was the social climate of the community? What role did your congregation play in promoting race relations in your community? What impact do you think that history plays on contemporary race relations in your community?

5. In Matthew 25:31–46, Jesus describes a King who separates people, just as a shepherd separates the sheep from the goats, based on their treatment of marginalized populations. In what ways are you a sheep or a goat?

Notes

[1] J. Barndt, Becoming an Anti-racist Church: Journeying Toward Wholeness (Minneapolis: Augsburg-Fortress, 2011).

[2] C. Carson, K. Shepard, & A. Young, A Call to Conscience: The Landmark Speeches of Dr. Martin Luther King, Jr. (New York: Warner Books, 2002). 28.

[3] Martin Luther King Jr., I Have a Dream: Writings and Speeches That Changed the World, Special 75th Anniversary Edition (San Francisco: Harper, 2003).

[4] Ibid.

[5] Ibid.

[6] Derald Wing Sue, "Microaggressions, Marginality and Oppression," in Microaggressions and Marginality, ed. D. W. Sue (Hoboken, NJ: Wiley, 2010), 3–22.

[7] Derald Wing Sue, C. Capodilupa, G. Torina, J. Bucceri, A. Holder, K. Nadal, M. Esquilin, "Racial Microaggressions in Everyday Life," American Psychologist 62,4 (2007): 271–286.

[8] Derald Wing Sue, Microaggressions and Marginality, 3.

[9] D. R. Williams, Y. Yu, J. S. Jackson, & N. B. Anderson, "Racial differences in physical and mental health: Socioeconomic status, stress, and discrimination," Journal of Health Psychology 2 (2003): 335–351.

[10] T. Evans-Campbell, "Historical Trauma in American Indian/Native Alaska Communities," Journal of Interpersonal Violence 23,3 (2008): 316–338.

[11] Derald Wing Sue, "Race Talk: The Psychology of Racial Dialogues. American Psychologist 68,8 (2013): 661–663.

[12] Yael Danieli, "Assessing Trauma Across Cultures from a Multigenerational Perspective," in J. P. Wilson and C. So-Kum Tang, ed. Cross-Cultural Assessment of Psychological Trauma and PTSD (New York: Springer, 2007): 65–87.

[13] M. Y. H. Brave Heart, "Gender Differences in the Historical Trauma Response Among the Lakota,"Journal of Health & Social Policy 10,4 (1999): 1–21.

[14] V. Rakoff, "A Long-term Effect on the Concentration Camp Experience," Viewpoints 1 (1966): 17–20 and Danieli, "Assessing Trauma."

[15] Yael Danieli, Cross-Cultural Assessment of Psychological Trauma and PTSD, 66.

[16] D. Nagata, S. Trierweiler, and R. Talbot, "Long-term Effects of Internment During Early Childhood in Third Generation Japanese Americans," American Journal of Orthopsychiatry 69,1 (1999): 19–29.

[17] D. Nagata, "International Effects of the Japanese American Internment," in International Handbook of Multigenerational Legacies of Trauma, ed. Y. Danieli (New York: Plenum Press, 1998): 125–139.

[18] T. Evans-Campbell, "Historical Trauma in American Indian/Native Alaska Communities," Journal of Interpersonal Violence 23,3 (2008): 37.

[19] Fred Gray, Bus Ride to Justice: Changing the System by the System, the Life and Works of Fred Gray Revised edition (Montgomery, AL: New South Books, 2013).

[20] B. Stevenson, Just Mercy: A Story of Justice and Redemption (New York: Spiegel & Grau, 2014).

[21] Ibid.

[22] William Edward Burghardt Du Bois, The Souls of Black Folk (Chicago: A.C. McClurg, 1903; New York, Bartleby.com, 1999) and; Stevenson, Just Mercy.

[23] Isabela Wilkinson, The Warmth of Other Suns: The Epic Story of America's Great Migration (New York: Random House, 2010).

[24] Yael Danieli, *Cross-Cultural Assessment of Psychological Trauma and PTSD*, 67.

[25] Derald Wing Sue, *Microaggressions in Everyday Life: Race, Gender, and Sexual Orientation* (Hoboken, NJ: John Wiley & Sons, 2010).

[26] P. Freire, *Pedagogy of the Oppressed* (New York: Herder and Herder, 1970), Sue, *Microaggressions in Everyday Life: Race, Gender, and Sexual Orientation*, and Sue et al, "Racial Microaggressions in Everyday Life," *American Psychologist* 62,4 (2007).

[27] Sue, "Microaggressions, Marginality and Oppression," in *Microaggressions and Marginality*, 11.

[28] Sue, et al. "Race Talk," *American Psychologist* 68,8 (2013): 666–667.

[29] Sue, *Microaggressions in Everyday Life: Race, Gender, and Sexual Orientation* and Sue, "Microaggressions, Marginality and Oppression," in *Microaggressions and Marginality*, 7.

[30] Martin Luther King Jr., *I Have a Dream: Writings and Speeches That Changed the World*, 68.

[31] "I Too, Am Harvard," accessed April 11, 2016, https://www.youtube.com/watch?v=uAMTSPGZRiI/. This exercise is adapted from Hatch workshops (http://media.sheknows.com/article-downloads/hatch-discussion-guide.pdf) designed to help parents discuss difficult topics with their children. Each video is available on YouTube. See also "The Invisible Discriminator," accessed April 11, 2016, https://www.youtube.com/watch?v=MvTyI41PvTk/.

The Art of Scapegoating and the Hard Work of a More Lasting Change

by David Fleer

Can We Talk?

EIGHTEEN MONTHS AGO RACIAL TURMOIL AND UNREST WERE beginning to broil on the national stage. Or at least among white folk, awareness of racial unrest and turmoil was arising. The dates and litany of names are now familiar:

Beginning in the summer of 2014:

- Eric Garner ~ July, New York
- Michael Brown ~ August, Ferguson
- Tamir Rice (a 12 year old child) ~ November, Cleveland

In 2015:

- Eric Harris ~ March, Oklahoma
- Walter Scott (shot eight times in the back) ~ April, North Charleston
- Freddie Gray ~ April, Baltimore

And then in June, 2015, a young Caucasian man walked into an African American church in Charleston and sat through a Bible study with Christians who welcomed him into their midst and invited his participation. After an hour of witnessing Christians at prayer and study, this white man responded with murder. Motivated by racist hatred, the man gunned down nine persons in cold blood . . . in church . . . as he uttered racist remarks and shouted: "You rape our women, you're taking over our country. You have to go."

Can we talk?

In the wake of the killing of nine African American worshipers at Emanuel AME Church pictures of the twenty one year old killer showed him draped with the confederate flag which stimulated politicians into action:

- South Carolina Republican Governor Nikki Haley demanded the legislature pass a measure removing the Confederate flag from the capitol grounds.
- Mississippi Senator Roger Wicker called for changing his state's flag that has been used since Reconstruction, saying it "should be put in a museum and replaced by one that's more unifying."
- Even Wal-Mart, Amazon, and Target leapt into action announcing they will no longer sell merchandise emblazoned with the confederate flag.

A flurry of action, but will anything happen beyond the removal of a symbol?

Can we talk?

And to think, just eighteen months ago, most white folk in America still believed that we were living in a "post racial America," that all we needed was to take Rodney King's words to heart, "Can't we all just get along?" and churches coming together once a year at a unity meeting was more than enough, "thank you very much for turning out."

Just a year ago, you could hear white folk say: "I have known blacks, I have worked with blacks, I went to school with blacks. Some of my best friends are black. Once we had a black lady clean our home and she became very close to our family. So, I am not a racist."

Just a year ago, you could hear young white folk say: "Racism is a problem for your generation, David. We millennials don't have that problem."

Meanwhile, the president and chancellor at the University of Missouri resigned as they were unable to address a rising number of racist incidents; many black students say that racial tensions are woven into the fabric of everyday life.

And, in Los Angeles the dean of students at prestigious Claremont McKenna College resigned in response to protests over her treatment of students of color.

Even today, tension and unrest is spreading to other colleges across the country and some are wisely calling for a national conversation on racism and injustice.

Can we, as people of faith, talk?

Where Do We Start?

We can begin by saying up front that the post racial America confidently pronounced seven years ago, stimulated by the election of President Barack Obama, was premature and ill-informed.

We can begin by confessing that Sunday morning, as always, is the most segregated hour in America, and church in some places is a bastion of racial resentment.

We can begin, as black Christians and white Christians gathered to "Advance the National Conversation on Race," by acknowledging that we have a rare opportunity, one that doesn't come often, but is now upon us.

We can begin by declaring:

- Racism, in all its nefarious expressions, personally and systemically, is a sin.
- Racism is a sin that needs to be revealed and exposed to the end that God may heal both church and society.

We can begin, by affirming:

- We believe in truth *and* reconciliation.
- We believe in truth *before* reconciliation.
- We believe we must tell the truth before we can even *think* of reconciliation.
- In academic terms, we believe truth telling is a *prerequisite* for reconciliation.

Why Can't I Take That Course?

"I want to take the course on reconciliation."

"Have you taken the prerequisite, the course on telling the truth?"

"No"

"Then you can't take the reconciliation course. The Truth course is a *prerequisite to reconciliation.*"

"I know there's a problem and I want to be part of the solution. I believe in reconciliation."

"That's good, but truth telling is a *prerequisite* for reconciliation."

Truth telling is the hardest course in the catalogue and nobody wants to take it. Some churches and colleges offer it only as an elective.

Why?

Because the truth can hurt.

Sometimes the truth makes people cry.

Sometimes the truth is hidden.

Sometimes we're the ones who've hidden the truth, even from ourselves.

So, if we're going to talk, let us resolve to tell the truth, first to ourselves and then to one another.

The Art of Scapegoating

The title of this section is: "A Lesson in Truth Telling: The Art of Scapegoating" and I take as my text, Leviticus 16: 8–10.

> *And Aaron shall cast lots for the two goats; one lot for the LORD and the other for the scapegoat. Aaron shall bring the goat whose lot falls to the LORD and sacrifice it for a sin offering.*

But the goat chosen as the scapegoat shall be presented alive before the LORD to be used for making atonement by sending it into the wilderness as a scapegoat.

And so it was in ancient Israel, on the Day of Atonement, two goats were chosen: one to be "The Lord's Goat" which was offered as a blood sacrifice, and the other, a scapegoat, to be sent away into the wilderness.

Since the second goat was sent out to the desert to perish, the word "scapegoat" has come to represent a person who is blamed and punished for the sins of others.

So the practice of ancient Israel has morphed and continues even today in our nation, in our churches and in our lives. There are so many exceptional scapegoats who parade before us today!

- The mess last fall with the owner of the Los Angeles Clippers. What was his name? Who can remember? We made him into a scapegoat and exiled him into the wilderness!
- The Louisiana congressman who spoke at a David Duke event in 2002 "not knowing about David Duke." Ha! Send him into the wilderness!

Scapegoats make themselves available to us every day.

For a white northerner, like me, raised in the '50s and '60s, the southern practice of Jim Crow is easy scapegoating:

- Dateline Georgia: "It shall be unlawful for any colored baseball team to play baseball in any vacant lot or baseball diamond within two blocks of any playground devoted to the white race."
- Dateline Tennessee: Separate buildings for black and white patients in hospitals for the insane.
- Dateline Oklahoma: At the very moment we are being launched into the afterlife, Blacks are not allowed to use the same hearse as whites.

The southern practice of Jim Crow is easy scapegoating.

White northerners, frankly, enjoy hearing these examples. White northerners are quick to explain, "Such are not the practices of those of us who are from (how shall we say?) 'the more sophisticated' regions of our nation. We are not racists."

Well . . . .

About the time Harding College, David Lipscomb College, and Abilene Christian College were (finally) allowing black students entry, Mrs. Warwick arrived as the new fourth grade teacher to my Lakeshore Elementary School in a Portland, Oregon suburb that had an African American population of less than 1%.

Mrs. Warwick was black.

I recently contacted my childhood friend, Bobby, who has a keen memory, and inquired about Mrs. Warwick, vaguely remembering some "dust up" that involved the teacher. Mrs. Warwick, as far as I can remember, was the only African American at Lake Shore Elementary in 1963.

Bobby wrote back:

> The only controversy I remember was my mom going up there and telling the powers that be that I wasn't going to be in Mrs. Warwick's class.
>
> When I was in the third grade I had Mrs. Halliday who went on leave and one of the subs was a black woman that scared the bejeebers [Bobby's language] out of me! I think that is probably why my mom didn't want me in the black fourth grade teacher's class. Her being big and black somehow scared me!

However, as I recall, Mrs. Warwick was of normal size and I've long felt my family morally superior to Bobby's (who has now become my new scapegoat).

Scapegoating is Common and Easy!

Jim Clark and Bull Connor, chiefs of police in Selma and Birmingham. Vicious dogs and fire hoses? Easy scapegoats!

My dad, a white northerner, was appalled by their behavior.

My dad, once in the military, for a short time was stationed at an Air Force base somewhere in the Deep South. He would tell the story that when he was in the South he walked right up to a drinking fountain labeled "colored" and he took a drink. He would then continue, "So, I'm no racist" (as if his drink of water proved his character). "I'm no racist, BUT . . . ."

And then my dad would unleash a racist opinion too foul and embarrassing to articulate in these pages.

But, watch what I've done: by identifying my own father's racism I make him into a scapegoat and send him into the wilderness, thinking I'm off the hook.

Well, dear reader, you may ask, "You scapegoat your childhood friend and your own father? Who won't you make into a scapegoat?"

The answer: nobody. There is no end to the quantity and quality of my scapegoats. Give me an opportunity and need and I might turn you into a scapegoat!

But, the problem with scapegoats is that we think they take away our sins. However, scapegoats don't take away our sins. Scapegoats only allow us to pretend we have no sin and push that sin down into a place where it can metastasize and spread through our blood and our minds into a sophisticated understanding that accepts racism in systems, economies, markets, and whole societies.

You will never find a sophisticated racist (like me) who uses the N word or turns fire hoses on innocent protesters or beats an unarmed woman with a billy club on the Edmund Pettus Bridge.

I would never say that a big black woman scared me.

I would never repeat my dad's hateful speech.

These are the behaviors of my scapegoats who allow me to turn a blind eye to the systemic racism that exists today, a systemic racism that works still to my advantage in real estate transactions, bank loans and even our Christian universities. How else can we explain, in 2016, the near all white presidencies and administrations at our Church of Christ related schools?

How do we even talk about such things when the most liberal white people we know are focused on scapegoats?

Soon after last year's release of the movie, Selma, George Wallace, Jr, wrote an essay, published in a conservative journal, claiming that the movie did not properly portray his father. Junior claimed that George Wallace, Sr had a contrite heart.

I read the article. . . Well, to be honest, I didn't read the entire article. I read only the first few sentences and then skimmed to the final paragraph where junior says that Oprah Winfrey and Jesse Jackson were at George Wallace's funeral.

Ha! I don't care if Pope Francis attended and Jesus officiated at the Governor's funeral. I'm not about to forgive him. I need George Wallace. He's my favorite scapegoat.

George Wallace, Foy E. Wallace Jr., and A. C. Pullias all too easily can become scapegoats from our past.

But, while we are not guilty of the sins they committed, let us not send them out into the wilderness lest we forget that while we today are not guilty of their sins, we are accountable for their actions. Scapegoating prevents us from seeing our accountability.

We believe in Truth and Reconciliation. We believe in Truth before Reconciliation. We believe Truth is a prerequisite to Reconciliation.

The Hard Work of More Lasting Change

It would be a betrayal . . . . if we allow ourselves to slip into a comfortable silence once the eulogies have been delivered, once the TV cameras move on. It would be a betrayal to go back to business as usual but that's what we so often do to avoid uncomfortable truths about the prejudice that still infects our society. To settle for symbolic gestures without following up with the hard work of more lasting change.

So warned our nation's president when he delivered the eulogy for Reverend Clement Pinckney and eight other members of Emanuel AME, all killed on June 17, 2015.

There might have been a rush to make Dylann Roof into our next scapegoat. He's such a perfect candidate. But he's been disqualified.

On the day that Dylann Roof appeared in court, family members of the murdered people were present. Some decided to speak directly to the accused, and Nadine Collier startled the courtroom when she said to Roof, "I forgive you, God have mercy on your soul." Her mother, Ethel Lance, had been one of his victims.

Alana Simmons, whose grandfather had been killed, stood up in the courtroom and said, "We are here to combat hate-filled actions with love-filled actions."

Despite their anger and pain, others offered forgiveness to the white supremacist.

The anguish, grace, and forgiveness of one family member after another stunned the world and claimed the front page headline of the next day's *New York Times.*

The family members' actions, perhaps too soon expressed, still set the tone for the conversation on race that now welcomes our participation and leadership.

The families want justice, of course, but the families are also saying that:

- Love is stronger than hate.
- Love must speak directly to hate.
- We must not make Dylann Roof into a scapegoat, as nefarious as his actions were.

But, do not be deceived. The opportunity for "accountability" and action now before us can easily slide into misdirection, inappropriate attention, and inaction. Opposition will be stiff and unyielding.

The stunning words of the Charleston families might be misinterpreted as a model of quick and easy forgiveness which denies the hard work of a more lasting change.

Opposition will be strong. During last November's protests on the campuses of Missouri, Yale University and elsewhere, the *Wall Street Journal* articulated a powerful counter attack. Featured as the *Journal's* major opinion piece, Roger Kimball ridiculed "The Rise of the College Crybullies."[1] Acknowledging that the news emanating from academia that week had the nation "mesmerized and appalled," Kimball claimed that "spurious charges of 'systemic racism,' 'a culture of rape' and sundry other imaginary torts compete for the budget of pity and special treatment" throughout higher education and, by implication, is all the nooks and crannies where black people are allowed to identify white privilege.

How do we respond to such a claim?

We can begin by *acknowledging our history*. Indeed, to make racial reconciliation possible, we must tell the truth, first to ourselves, and then to one another. This is the hard work of a more lasting change.

We can begin by *reminding ourselves that scapegoats blind us to the systemic racism that cripples our land*. This is the hard work of a more lasting change.

We can look *beyond persons cloaked in white robes and spewing racial epithets and open our minds to the systems that have historically, and to this day, restricted black men and women in all American cities.*

Such acts of "accountability" identify the venues for the hard work of a more lasting change.

When hearts are open and conversations are respectful and honest, God can break down walls and reach across divides. We can put beliefs into action. We are capable and prepared for the hard work of a more lasting change.

I've delivered some variation of this address one dozen times in twelve cities and six states, at the Racial Unity Leadership Summits, in sermonic form and before citywide racial unity meetings. But now, in this volume, for those of us gathered to "Advance the National Conversation on Race," knowing that the opportunity before us is both rare and challenging, this essay, assembled with the others in this volume, is a call to *action*.

May God grant us the courage to talk about the things that matter most. To use biblical language, to speak of those things of first importance, the second greatest commandment, "to love your neighbor as yourself," and the "weightier matters" that Jesus defined as "justice, faithfulness and mercy."

May God grant us wisdom and courage to tell the truth.

No scapegoating. No evading the issues. But, determined as people of faith, to do the hard work that might bring a more lasting change. This time, joined together as black and white, may God use the church as a "headlight" and not "taillight" to bring to the communities where we live the more lasting change we long for: racial reconciliation.

Discussion Questions

1. Nominate one recent candidate for "Scapegoat for Racial Injustice." Identify this person's characteristics that make him or her the ideal nominee.

2. The author claims the post racial America confidently pronounced seven years ago, stimulated by the election of President Barack Obama, was "premature and ill informed." Do you agree? Why or why not?

3. When the author spoke of his own "sophisticated racism" what instances came to your mind?

4. Identify from your experience or in your community one example of "systemic racism."

5. What are the actions most needed in your community that can bring about "The Hard Work of a More Lasting Change"?

Notes

[1] Roger Kimball, "The Rise of the College Crybullies," *The Wall Street Journal*, Saturday/Sunday (November 14 – 15, 2015): A9.

The Centered Church

by Don McLaughlin

A LEADER IN OUR CHURCH HAS THE RESPONSIBILITY TO SET UP, staff, train, and monitor customer call centers for a large United States power company. The call center strategy is used by businesses large and small all over the world to provide a centralized and consistent response to problems experienced by their customers. Pastors serving in the majority of churches often find themselves serving as the call center for the church. They field calls that range from complaints about the clogged sink in the ladies' room to questions about the theology of human suffering. Their members have expectations about how the pastor should or should not respond.

This system is a tightrope walk for the pastor. The food on the pastor's table is directly related to his or her ability to meet the needs (expectations) of the customer base . . . better known as the church members. Depending on the social and financial pressure a member may be able to leverage, a pastor may struggle to speak boldly against the oppressive powers or systemic abuses in society.

As I was typing this paragraph, a young pastor called me with a heavy heart. He shared that since he began preaching about how the gospel confronts systematic racism in his community, support among the leaders and members was wavering. He wondered aloud with me if he needed to start looking for another church. The phone was ringing off the hook in the call center (aka—the church office), and he was faced with moving from the center (Christ) or moving his family.

He is not alone. Although there are definitely signs of hope for greater cultural and racial integration in the North American church, over 90 percent of U.S. churches are still ethnically and culturally homogenous. Many talk about wanting things to change, but few are willing to pay the price. As usual, the church is following society rather than confronting and transforming it. Churches in North America have almost no influence on society in regard to improving multi-racial, multi-ethnic and multi-cultural relationships. But are we content to leave it this way? I am not, and I imagine that if you are reading this essay neither are you.

I believe the church is central to what God is doing in his world. No institution on the planet is better suited or positioned to make a difference in regard to reconciliation that the church. In this brief essay, I want to outline how I believe this can be done. I hope to make my case with stories, Scripture, and common sense application. I intend to include real problems, barriers, and traps we face along the way, but none of these are insurmountable.

The Context for Our Story

I serve as the preaching minister in a beautiful church, or what many call a "faith family." We are located in Atlanta, Georgia and have around 1,200 members. Of this number, a little over 50 percent are white of mostly European descent, around 40 percent are black of African descent, and the remaining 10 percent include several ethnicities, but mostly a thriving Latino contingent. Since its earliest days, the church has always been seen as "inclusive" and accepting. This was never one of "those" churches that excluded people because of skin color or ethnicity. The local and international mission work was multicultural, whether in the former Soviet Union, an African country, or Central America. By the late '80s and early '90s, the church had already ordained a black elder, had a few black deacons, and had a black preacher-in-training on staff. This was considered progressive even for Atlanta at the time. But at our core, we were still a white, affluent, politically conservative, and a (culturally) Southern church.

In the late '90s, God began writing a new chapter in our story: *intentional integration*. Although I would like to say we were all aware and onboard with what God was doing, we were not. God was at work in ways that would only manifest themselves as the process unfolded. So what exactly did happen that grew us from being a church that was 95 percent white and culturally dominated by white, Southern, affluence to a church of such diversity?

Read This Story . . . Again!

Donna gave me an article to read. She is African-American and the wife of one of our elders. The article, written by the wife of a Supreme Court judge, was about being "colorblind." When I reported back to Donna that I had finished the article she asked me, "Well, what do you think?" I answered that I thought the article was great. She replied, "That's the problem. The article isn't great." So I asked her to explain, and she simply told me, "You go back and read it again and try to see why there is a problem with this kind of thinking." So I did. I read the article again, equipped with the awareness that people of color could see this through a different lens. My eyes were opened to something I had not considered: to be "colorblind" means that if I was to notice your color, the outcome would be negative. Why else would we encourage colorblindness? We would never consider going through a rose garden wishing that all the roses were gray. We wouldn't say to a man or woman, "I'm gender blind . . . I don't even notice gender." Inherent in the statement, "I don't even notice color," is the idea that "I don't see YOU." God is not colorblind. God is colorful, and his creation abundantly bears witness. Color is beautiful whether it is a rose, a sunset, or our skin. So I made an immediate shift in my thinking to abandon the concept of being colorblind and to embrace being colorful.

Table Conversations

God, then, introduced me to Jerry Taylor in 2001. He and his wife and two children were a part of our church for a few years. Jerry is an amazing friend, brother, and conversation partner. One afternoon Jerry and I met in my office. We were talking about issues of diversity and shared life.

I said to Jerry:

1. There are questions I want to ask, but I do not know how to ask them.
2. There are words that I will use that I do not know are offensive unless someone tells me.
3. There are questions I think are important, but they are not.
4. Conversely, there are questions I do not think are important that are actually essential.
5. I want to know what African-Americans talk about when no white people are around. What are the concerns, frustrations, joys, hopes and dreams that are shared around the "black table" when white people are not present?

Then I asked a final question: "Jerry, will you be that conversation partner with me?" He agreed, and we have been inseparable since. Jerry is one of the most influential people in our nation right now in regard to race and reconciliation. He founded the Racial Unity Leadership Summit, a nationwide initiative to bring churches into constructive and transformative conversations around race and reconciliation. Jerry and I talked for over five hours in that first conversation, closing our time together on our knees in prayer.

Everyone needs conversation partners who will help them grow in this approach to transformative dialogue. What started with Jerry became a template for conversations surrounding other arenas ripe for reconciliation, such as gender equality, immigration, politics, gay rights, education and health reform, etc. We need people to walk, talk, and listen with us who will not give up when we are struggling through delicate subjects.

Tell Me More...

We read and hear a chorus of lament in America right now over the toxic nature of public and private discourse. From our presidential race to church business meetings, respect and common decency seem to have been abandoned. We simply do not practice listening with patience, thoughtful reflection, and humility. The issues surrounding systemic racism evoke strong emotional responses. It seems that we are all wearing our feelings on our sleeves just waiting to be offended. We are emotionally frail and psychologically brittle. "Venting" has become socially acceptable. An entire industry with its own emerging vocabulary has grown up with social media where we can "like," someone's post, or reply with an "emoticon," to punctuate our response. Perhaps most troubling in this development is the lack of differentiation between the behaviors of those who claim Jesus as Lord and those who do not. People can "unfriend" those who "offend" them too much. This online, isolated behavior can go "viral" and ruin someone's life overnight.

But what is lacking is a "listening" icon that says to others, "tell me more." Listening well is an adult behavior, and as my daughter in her mid-twenties likes to say, "Adulting is hard!" But how can we make the most of our table conversations if we do not have the emotional and psychological stamina to listen well?

A key example of this came out in the aftermath of the death of Freddie Gray in Baltimore. Politicians and newscasters used the word "thug" to describe those who were demonstrating against systemic racism in policing practices. To the average white person, this word seemed appropriate for the actions they were observing. But it was only after some African-Americans began discussing how the word "thug" had become a term with negative racial connotations did whites sit up and take notice. And then a divide, typical of our culture erupted. Some mocked the concern and used "thug" all the more with their sense of righteous indignation. Others appreciated and respected the conversation as helpful and constructive. The difference in the responses seems to be linked to maturity, empathy and humility.

These events and conversations taking place in the public arena informed us as a church. We hosted a "listening" seminar for our leadership, training them to listen well and create space for others to share different and even opposing views without reprise or interruption. This has proven to be critically important to building healthy, intentional integration in our church.

Do I Have to Know You Less to Love You More?

Coming directly on the heels of our growth in table conversations and listening skills was the question posed here: "Do I have to know you less to love you more?" Much like the implications between colorful versus colorblind, we faced head on the question of assimilation versus integration. Stated more plainly, did our black members have to "act white" to fit in? When I would ask our members of color about this, there was an initial hesitancy. That simple hesitation was answer enough, but I wanted more . . . more understanding . . . more nuance . . . more insight.

One of our elders, Fernando, has been an amazing and faithful friend and conversation partner. He often suggests books and articles for me to read that can give me background and context to the nature of systemic racism. At his encouragement, I read *Souls of Black Folk* wherein the author, W. E .B. Du Bois articulates "double-consciousness." An excerpt could be beneficial:

> "Between me and the other world there is ever an unasked ques-
> tion: . . . How does it feel to be a problem? . . . One ever feels
> his two-ness,—an American, a Negro; two souls, two thoughts,
> two unreconciled strivings; two warring ideals in one dark body,
> whose dogged strength alone keeps it from being torn asunder."[1]

When applied to the church, it is inconsistent with the Gospel of Jesus that anyone should have to endure such anguish to find love, respect and full fellowship in their local church (Galatians 2). One should not have to hide a part of themselves to experience the love, compassion, acceptance, joy and sweet fellowship at the table of the Savior in the midst of his family.

The Church of the Nativity

God began to impress on us the nature and impact of his earthly presence in and through the church. Scripture revealed this consistent theme throughout. We noticed for the first time the diversity of the "church of the nativity." When you study the extended birth story of Jesus, you see an amazing gathering around Jesus of the diversity pictured in heaven. Consider this:

1. *Economic Diversity:* The Wise Men are so wealthy they can travel a great distance, offload gifts of great monetary value, and still have plenty to return to their country of origin. Along with them you have Zechariah and Elizabeth (parents of John the Baptist) who are also "white collar" folk. But then you have the blue collar of a carpenter (Joseph) and the "no-collar" shepherds. The poorer estate of Joseph and Mary in comparison to the Wise Men is noted in their offering of two turtle-doves instead of a lamb at Jesus' consecration at the temple (this being an acceptable offering for the poor).
2. *Family Structure Diversity*: In this story you have an older couple (Zechariah and Elizabeth) who finally have their only child. But you also have a young pregnant girl with her "not-married-long-enough-to-be-the-father" husband, and an elderly widow (Anna).
3. *The Wise Men from the East* were most likely Persian (modern-day Iranian), and their skin would have certainly been noticeably darker than the others in the narrative.
4. *Educationally,* the Wise Men (perhaps men of science or astrology) represent the top of the educational ladder in the story, followed perhaps by John the Baptist's parents and Simeon, the man holding to God's promise that seeing the Christ would precede his death. But history bears witness that most of the others in the story were more than likely barely literate as far as formal education goes.

You may see other forms of the diversity in the story, but what is the significance of this detailed account? All of them were called by God to participate in this story! Either through dreams, a miraculous star, visions, angel visits, or the Holy Spirit each of them was specifically recruited and "cast" for their role. God could have chosen anyone or no one to surround his son in Bethlehem, but it is significant that this collection of humanity is a template for the mission of Christ. He is consistently moving among the diverse peoples around him, breaking down barriers and smashing traditional walls of exclusion, oppression, and prejudice.

The Lord's Prayer and Heaven's Presence

Jesus' model prayer (Matt. 6:9–13) coupled with the vision of heaven's house of worship (Rev. 7:9–15) coalesced into a mandate for diversity: Around the throne in heaven is a "great multitude that no one could count from every nation, tribe, people, and language" in worship to God and in fellowship with each other. Jesus taught us to pray, "Your kingdom come, your will be done *on earth as it is in heaven*," and you have our mandate. The church, right now on earth, is to be a witness to heaven's spiritual *and* social environment.

Once Born and Twice Born

In John 3, we overhear the gospel proclamation in a conversation between Jesus and Nicodemus. Jesus articulates to Nicodemus that though all are once-born, there is a new birth from above that ushers people into the kingdom of God. Those born from above are the twice born, birthed by the Spirit. Twice-born people crystalize their lives around the person and work of Jesus Christ. As they are centered on Christ, these twice-born people discover each other, and together they build the body of Christ. But what is this body to be like?

The Great Commission

This spirit and mandate of diversity is cemented in the Great Commission (Matt. 28:18–20) and even more clearly articulated in Acts 1:8. The miracle of Pentecost isn't the tongues of fire but the tongues of nations. With breathtaking boldness, this gospel theme drives the early church. The commitment to all the widows in Acts 6 and the embrace of the Samaritans and Africans in Acts 8 are precursors to the ultimate step of accepting Gentiles on even footing with the Jews beginning with Acts 10. This non-negotiable of mutuality consumes the rest of Acts and the letters of Paul. There will be one church of all and no church for some. The elect will be the one family of God through the blood of Christ not the elite family of a race through the blood of man.

The Great Command

Paul's letters are theologically and practically stuffed with the "ministry of reconciliation." The work of Jesus on the cross was not just a ticket to an eternal home on the blissful shore by and by! Jesus had done something on the cross that would change the way people live right now. This is not the social gospel as some would name it, but rather, it is how the gospel changes the society. The gospel confronts the social order of sinful flesh. In his body on the cross, Jesus destroys the dividing wall that separated person from person. His intent was to create one new man in himself, thus making peace. All reconciled to God are reconciled to each other.

James the half-brother of Jesus carries this same theme into his letter, noting that one cannot be faithful to the glorious Lord if one is not faithful to the "other" among us. John adds his own exclamation point when he writes that one's love of God is only authenticated by one's tangible love for fellow humans.

There is simply no escaping that all barriers that turn humans against each other or even away from each other are NOT of God—period—and have no place in the church. In order to build the kind of fellowship that bears witness to the unifying work of Jesus Christ in the world, we had to learn how to have substantive conversations about extremely difficult issues. Perhaps the most difficult of these conversations is the meaning and impact of white privilege and how a dominant culture can actually creep into the environment of the local church.

Access to All, Privilege to None

Through Jesus we all have *access* to the Father by the Spirit. The veil that served as a representative of the dividing wall of hostility was torn asunder so that all people would be joined together. It was God's intent through the church that the powers and principalities know that God's redemptive power was greater than the world's divisive schemes. Therefore, what God has joined together let no man put asunder.

White Americans, including white Christians, often bristle at a discussion of privilege. When "white privilege" is discussed, most whites do not appreciate the supposed insinuation. It is necessary for any and all churches that intend to share their lives and worship across all cultures and colors to have productive discussions about privilege. There are majority cultures in nearly every nation of the world. This means that from country to country the privileged culture may be wrapped in a different color skin or speak a different language. But privilege is at the core of what the gospel of Jesus Christ seeks to remove, so it must be explored.

First, privilege does not have to do with assets or resources; but rather, it has to do with *access*. In the United States of America, the demographic that enjoys the highest level of unrestricted access is white European. Let me offer some examples that may help us understand this.

1. *Homer Plessy—New Orleans, Louisiana*
   Homer Plessy was born during the Civil War and became famous as an adult in the United States Supreme Court case known as Plessy vs. Ferguson. Although Homer received a brief taste of integration in the post-war South, it was short-lived. He had a fair complexion but was 1/8 black, which categorized him as a "Negro." Homer, *because of his complexion*, could have freely boarded any train car in his day, even those designated "whites only," but he believed this to be unjust. In 1892, he purchased a first-class ticket and sat in the whites-only section. He was arrested as part of a plan to bring the segregationist laws before the court. Judge John Howard Ferguson, however, denied his rights, and this set the case on a track that ended up in the Supreme Court. The Court had started leaning more toward segregation, and in 1896 handed down what became infamously known as the "Separate but Equal" ruling. This enshrined

segregation in the legal code of the nation. A sad day indeed, and
it would be nearly sixty more years until it would be struck down.

2. *Robert E. Jones—Mississippi*

   Jones was the first African-American General Superintendent
   of the AME Church. While speaking at a retreat for white
   Christians in Ohio, Jones came up with the idea of establishing a
   retreat where blacks could attend. This was 1923 and the church,
   like the nation, was strictly segregated. In the South, blacks were
   not allowed access to public beaches with whites. Jones found
   a beautiful site on the Gulf Coast in Waveland, Mississippi.
   Although the locals would not consider selling the land to a black
   person, they sold the land to Jones *thinking he was white because
   of his light complexion.* Make sure you read that last sentence
   again. The whites would not sell the land to a black person, they
   sold it to Jones because they thought he was white!

3. *Walter White—President of the NAACP 1931–1955*

   White's story is absolutely fascinating. He was a dynamic leader
   with relentless energy and a keen mind for mobilizing people to
   a cause. Following his own description of himself, *White looked
   white.* He had blonde hair and blue eyes. Of his thirty-two great-
   great-great grandparents, five were black and twenty-seven were
   white. How would this categorize someone racially? While White
   was in Arkansas investigating the lynching of blacks, he over-
   heard whites of European decent pledging to kill him, and they
   noted that he was a "yellow n-gger" trying to pass as a white man.
   But those hunting for White didn't realize he was right there
   in their midst because he didn't look black. His *appearance as
   a white man* sheltered him from the violence other blacks were
   facing. Others complained that he wasn't "truly" black. But in
   1924, the Racial Integrity Act had been passed, codifying into
   law the 'One-Drop Rule." The one-drop (of blood) rule sought
   to legally bind all US Americans into either the "white" or "colored" categories at birth. One drop of black blood (five black

great-great-great grandparents in the case of Walter White) would legally classify him as Negro. These laws were in effect until overturned in 1967 by the US Supreme Court.

4. *George McLaurin—University of Oklahoma*

   In 1948, George applied to the law school at the University of Oklahoma and was denied. The school cited segregation laws, but the Supreme Court ruled in 1950 that the University of Oklahoma had to admit McLaurin to class. The school acquiesced, but seated McLaurin in an ante-room, separated from the rest of the students who were white. George McLaurin was fifty-four years old and had already earned his master's degree in education when he was denied *access* to the University of Oklahoma.

5. *Linda Brown—Topeka, Kansas*

   Linda Brown was a third-grader when her father Oliver joined the class-action lawsuit against the Board of Education. Along with the other plaintiffs, Brown simply wanted shared education. He wanted his daughter to be able to attend the elementary school that was nearest to their residence rather than being transported across town to a racial segregated school. The Supreme Court ruled in favor of the plaintiffs, striking down the "Separate but Equal" ruling nearly sixty years earlier in Plessy vs. Ferguson.

6. *Ruby Bridges—New Orleans, Louisiana*

   November 14, 1960, six year old Ruby Bridges was the only student to enter the William Frantz Elementary school. She was six years old. The Supreme Court had already struck down segregation in public schools some six years earlier, but many states and locales were not in compliance with the federal law. Many state and local leaders in Louisiana were committed to segregation, and it would take the federal government and troops to escort Ruby to the school which was legally *accessible* to her. The famous American artist, Norman Rockwell captured the emotion of the day and determination of Ruby in his classic work, "The Problem We All Live With."

7. *James Meredith—Mississippi*

Meredith was a nine-year veteran of the United States Air Force and had achieved good grades during his two years at Jackson State University when he applied for entrance to the University of Mississippi. It required a Supreme Court decision, pressure from the Attorney General of the United States, and 500 US Marshalls to enroll Meredith and seat him in a classroom October 1, 1962. Why would a veteran of the United States military, especially one who demonstrated academic acumen in two years at another state-accredited college ever be denied *access* to a public university?

I highlight these examples, but they represent millions (yes, *millions*) of experiences. All of these examples share a common thread: *privilege did not have to do with assets or resources, but with access.* In the famous case of the sit-ins at the lunch counter in the Greensboro, North Carolina Woolworth store (1960), four college freshman chose to demonstrate against segregation. This case was a landmark in the Civil Rights Movement as it highlighted the white privilege of *access*. In this case, the wealthiest black person in Greensboro was barred from service at the "whites only" lunch counter while the poorest white, if present with a nickel could sit down and buy a cup of coffee.

There are two primary reasons many whites chafe at the idea of white privilege. First, it offends their sense of being upright and fair, casting a demeaning embarrassment on their sense of personhood. It feels to them like being white is inherently bad. Secondly, whites react negatively against the idea of white privilege because they believe it belittles their own hardships, struggles, poverty and challenges. It is as if all their accomplishments were handed to them, and their hard work in overcoming their unique struggles would be downplayed. Doesn't everyone have to rise above life's tests?

This was highlighted in an August, 2014 interview with television personality Bill O'Reilly. He spoke passionately about his "hardscrabble life" growing up in Levittown, New York. He noted that his personal story "proved" that white privilege is a construct of liberals who are making damaging excuses for blacks not to succeed. But one only has to do a little research to learn of the white's only history of Levittown, leading to generational wealth and equity that was denied to blacks because of race. O'Reilly's argument proves the exact opposite of his claims. The fact that blacks were denied the opportunity to rent or own homes in the post-WWII explosion of the American suburban expansion absolutely gave whites a leg up, and it continues to generate economic inequity. Bill O'Reilly does, however highlight the struggles whites have to feel validated for their own accomplishments *while also* admitting their privileged status.

Both of these concerns are valid and should be taken seriously.

1. White privilege is not an attack on white people for being white.
2. White privilege is not an attempt to make white people feel guilty for having white skin. No one should bear an unequal burden for their skin color, right?
3. White privilege does not demean the hardships of anyone, and certainly does not belittle the poverty that many whites experience(d).

White privilege does, however, exist. It exists in the form of what author Peggy McIntosh termed, "The Invisible Knapsack." It means that the white culture in America is born into and is the dominant culture. This status means that in our country a white (male, and gender bias is a discussion for another time) person was offered citizenship while blacks were denied. Whites were never denied access to a school, higher education, or the political process based on the color of their skin. White people were not excluded from stores, restaurants, beaches, public parks, toilets, or drinking fountains because of their skin. Because of this access, whites were exposed to experiences and opportunities for many generations that give them invisible advantages that allow them to navigate many circumstances that others without these privileges cannot.

I have been criticized many times for speaking and writing on these issues. I have been directly accused, and even hit in the head with a purse, for "stirring up old issues that are no longer relevant." But it has always been white people that have declared that these issues are "old" or "fixed" in America. The last twenty-four months (2014–15) made it clear, from Ferguson to Baltimore, that "this ain't fixed!"

Whites want to isolate these cases as individual events so that they can discount them case-by-case. They want to find something in each case that suggests that the outcome, such as in the case of Michael Brown is really his fault. Many whites do not understand the Black Lives Matter movement because they do not see the connection between Trayvon, Eric, Michael, Tamir, Freddie, and a seemingly endless list. My wife and I have four sons and one daughter, including an African-American adopted son. Through our son, we have been made painfully aware of the ongoing systemic racism that plagues our society. And as the nation confronts these situations from different points of view, politics are woven into the equation, often resulting in an even greater divide. Whites can make a huge difference by respecting, and not discounting the voices from minority communities that attempt to shed light on their experiences in a white-dominated system.

So Can a Church Do This?

Yes! The church . . . *the intentionally integrated church*, can speak a fresh message of life, hope and redemption into this fractured world. The core message of the gospel levels the playing field. Our *shared access* to God through the work of Christ on the cross and the presence of the Holy Spirit destroys the barriers and the hostility. The love God gave us flows through us to each other. We do not fear each other because we know and love each other. Every syllable of the gospel message unifies the body of Christ into a colorful display of the creative heart of our Creator. This gospel message is centered in Christ and decenters any privileged group. The gospel destabilizes all systems that grant privileged access to power and resources.

Yes! The church that is willing to take tangible steps toward intentional integration can make a difference, and we have learned that the rays of hope must be wrapped in practical steps.

1. *Hospitality Challenge:* We recognize that worshiping together
   doesn't equate to relationships. We challenged every member in
   our church to have a meal with another member in their home
   . . . no restaurants allowed! This pressed us to share table time
   together in each other's space. As we continued this challenge
   over the years, the familiar structures of systemic segregation
   have continued to fall into irrelevance. As Jesus makes room (is
   hospitable) to all of us, so we make room for each other. When
   Jesus is at the center of the table, there is always room for all.

2. *Integrated Leadership:* If leadership and decision-making power
   is not shared, the church is NOT integrated. Our pastoral staff
   enjoys the distinct advantage of diversity with African-American,
   Latino, Asian and European men and women serving together.
   Our eldership is still heavy on the European demographic, but
   we do have two black elders and one Latino elder. But this is also
   significant. One of the hidden problems of systemic racism is
   shutting minorities out of the leadership development process. If
   you want a more diverse leadership you must open all the doors
   along the way that will contribute to their growth and experience.
   In October 2014, we ordained our first Latino elder. Significantly,
   Spanish is his primary language and his English is a work-in-
   progress. Not only did this impact the way the church saw leadership, but it shifted the pronouns in our Latino members from
   "them" to "us." When Jesus is the center of our leadership, there is
   no "them" among "us."

3. *Small Groups and Discipleship Models:* Our twenty-plus year
   commitment to intentional integration exposed tenacious pock-
   ets of systemic segregation. We determined to intentionally equip
   our small groups for diversity. This does include recruiting leaders and hosts from diverse demographics, but more specifically
   it equips these leaders to create environments where integration
   can flourish. This means leaders learn how to facilitate safe conversations that welcome and affirm diverse points of view concerning the application of Biblical teachings to complex social

concerns. It means purposefully getting to know each other in the small group so that we don't perpetuate assumptions about family, community, education, economics, and politics that affirm only one dominant culture. When our small groups are centered on knowing Christ and being transformed into his likeness, the reasonable and expected outcome is the blending of our shared lives.

4. *Worship:* You know the challenge churches face in regard to worship styles even when the membership is homogenous, so you can only imagine the size of the challenge with diversity! But once again, we have found this to be a gift in disguise. Many people assume that all whites prefer country, classical or rock music, and all blacks prefer hip hop, rap, or jazz! This couldn't be further from the truth! Worship has given us a shared language where God and his mission in the world are the preferred language, style and genre. The physical presence of diversity actually sets an expectation for diversity in worship. This doesn't solve all the worship frustrations, but diversity in worship is a blessing, not a curse. When God and his glory is the center of our praise, then the vision of Revelation 7 becomes the reality of our gatherings on earth.

As I close my thoughts, Jesus, only and always, is at the center of the church . . . his faith family. The call goes out from him, and as he is lifted up, he calls all people to himself. All who respond to his call meet each other at the center and become inextricably integrated with each other. There is NO other arrangement that qualifies for the label church of Christ.

Discussion Questions:

1. What is the value of a conversation partner on this journey towards racial reconciliation?

2. Could your congregational leadership benefit from a "listening seminar" as described by the author? Who should participate in this seminar?

3. Describe your congregation along the following characteristics:

    a. Economic Diversity
    b. Family Structure Diversity
    c. Racial Diversity
    d. Educational Diversity

Notes

[1]Du Bois, William Edward Burghardt. "Strivings of the Negro People – 1897.08." *The Atlantic Monthly*. Accessed April 5, 2016. http://www.theatlantic.com/past/unbound /flashbks/black/dubstriv.htm. DuBois, William Edward Burghardt. *The Souls of Black Folk: Essays and Sketches,* reprint edition (New York: Dover Publications 1994) (originally published by A.C. McClurg and Co.), 1–2.

Wednesday Work

A Conflict Manager's Thoughts on Pilgrimage Towards Reconciliation

by Phyllis Hildreth

Six women. Three men. Nine people, eighty-seven to twenty-six years of age. Five of them pastors; one, a state senator. The nine died in Wednesday worship. The nine were Christian. Nine Christians were martyred in worship. The nine were African-American.

THEY WERE SHOT TO DEATH BY A WHITE MALE WHOM THEY INVITED to worship with them, murdered in the church founded by Denmark Vesey, who, in 1821, began organizing enslaved persons towards rebellion. On Wednesday, June 17th, these men and women were massacred by a white gunman in a black church in southern city over which the confederate flag still flew.

The year was 2015. The name of the city is Charleston. The name of the church is Emanuel African Methodist Episcopal Church.

The names of the slain are:

Sharonda Coleman-Singleton	Clementa Pinckney
Cynthia Hurd	Tywanza Sanders
Susie Jackson	Daniel Simmons Sr.
Ethel Lance	Myra Thompson
DePayne Middleton-Doctor	

The name of the gunman will not be privileged here. But it could be argued that he did not act alone. For purposes of this conversation, let us assume his accomplices are legion. Their name is racism.

On Friday June 19th the accused gunman appeared in court for a bond hearing. Family members of several of the slain were present. In open court, on the record, many addressed the defendant. And forgave him, as did Nadine Collier, the daughter of seventy-year-old Ethel Lance. According to Washington Post journalist Mark Berman, she "said at the hearing, her voice breaking with emotion. 'You took something very precious from me. I will never talk to her again. I will never, ever hold her again. But I forgive you. And have mercy on your soul.'"[1]

Friday forgiveness. Breathtaking in its speed and magnitude. Almost as unfathomable as that other Friday, when another preacher, nearly-but-not-yet murdered, asked mercy for his killers (Luke 23:34). Many found Ms. Collier's forgiveness troubling not only because it seemed to be untimely but also unearned and unfair. In her June 22, 2015 article in *The New Republic*, Christian ethicist Elizabeth Stoker Bruenig explains:

> On the one hand, the Christian compulsion to forgive is
> absolute: and as exemplars of the faith, the families of the
> Charleston victims are excellent. On the other hand, their
> forgiveness presents a challenge to the onlooking public: are we
> ignoring their wishes if we do not join them in forgiving [the
> killer]? And what becomes of the discussion of the massacre
> if the rhetoric turns primarily to forgiveness? Further, why
> is it always black Christians who are burdened with the
> task of unilateral forgiveness without expectation of radical
> transformation? (Take, for instance, invocations of Martin

Luther King Jr.'s Christian example when the pitch of racial
tension rises high enough to worry moneyed interests.)

There is perhaps a second source of unease surrounding [the
killer]'s forgiveness, namely that he has shown not even a vague
sign of remorse, which makes the victims' families' decision to
forgive him seem all the more harrowing.[2]

Harrowing. It is harrowing indeed to stand at this incendiary intersection of
race, religion, and repetitive trauma and speak into a conversation between
white and black Christians on reconciliation. It is harrowing to face and
feel the anger, pain, and fear with which we are left. There is reluctance
to engage this conversation openly, blindly; not knowing who is listening
or how it will be received. The conflict manager's reluctance stems from
professional and practical knowledge that the path from breach to reconciliation is rarely direct, immediate, simple, or cheap. Rather, it is a journey;
sequenced, navigated, oft-times impeded by obstacles, some of which are
surmountable; others, only by miracle.

Steve Joiner, Managing Director of the Institute for Conflict Management
at Lipscomb University, and a leading practitioner in the field of congregational conflict, tells graduate students that clients only seek his help after
"running the bus into a ditch, turning it over, and setting it on fire." The
trauma and terror of unexpected and incendiary events tends to drive folk
to seek immediate assistance from the nearest available first responder.
Often, mere proximity to such events, real or perceived, triggers instincts
for protection and prevention, leading not only the crash victims, but also
second and third waves of the cautious and concerned to seek help.

So it is with outbreaks of social conflict based in race, especially when
the conflicts and consequences touch churches and congregations. It does
not matter whether the threat comes from racially motivated attacks upon
the church, racial tension within the church, or structural racism engulfing
communities beyond the church walls. Folk are hurting. The bus is in the
ditch and people are looking for a way out and a way forward. This essay
is one conflict manager's response to the call for reconciliation, the request
for roadside assistance in getting there. It is offered from the perspective

of the tow-truck driver tasked with getting the travelers unstuck, helping them recalculate a way forward, and pointing them in the general direction of the hoped-for destination.

This essay conceives of the black and white Christians reconsidering reconciliation as travelers on a journey that is something of a hybrid between conflict resolution process and holy pilgrimage. It proceeds without knowing when or where their journey began, who is on the bus, or where they thought they were going. It proceeds, however from the premise that, effective June 17, 2015, all roads pass through Charleston; all traffic stops at Emanuel A.M.E. Church. It suggests that no one is going anywhere until the damage done there is acknowledged, assessed, understood, and accounted for in the revised itinerary. First, it offers working definitions for conflict analysis. Next, it introduces a framework for mapping identity, agency, and equity in order to both locate damage in need of repair and resilient strength upon which to build. Also, it highlights a few tenets of conflict resolution praxis and suggest process parallels to travel narratives in biblical texts and spiritual practice. Finally, process landmarks of purification, preparation, presence, and persistence are suggested as predicates for, or on ramp towards reconciliation.

Exploring the Breach

Clearly marked definitions are indispensable guides through conflict. Like the pulsing blue ball on an electronic map, they can tell us where we are in relation to others. They can alert us to scale and orders of magnitude, useful for distinguishing between mountains and molehills. And when agreed upon as standard or authoritative, a definition itself is a powerful tool for resolving conflict. For this conversation, conflict may be defined as "an expressed struggle between at least two interdependent parties who perceive incompatible goals, scarce resources, and interference from the other party in achieving their goals."[3]

Social conflict arises when persons or groups believe they have incompatible social goals and act to protect against, suppress, damage or destroy the other. According to sociologists Kriesberg and Dayton, social conflicts tend to share these five hallmarks:

1. Social conflicts are not unusual, and not necessarily negative. They can occur with natural growth and change; they can signal problems that need to be corrected.
2. Social conflicts can be expressed with different levels of force or destructiveness—anything from strong language and raised voices to economic pressure (voting with one's checkbook) to divisiveness, violence.
3. Social conflict produce competing narratives. Each side tends to claim identities and brand its own story as to what happened, why it happened, and who is to blame.
4. Social conflicts escalate through identifiable stages. Disputes may begin with frustrated attempts at problem-solving, progress though disagreement, proceed to ineffective negotiation, broken trust, accelerate to aggressive competition, power-based coercion, towards ultimate destruction.
5. Social conflicts can be transformed. Conflict escalation may be slowed, halted, or reversed through processes that acknowledge harm, render fair and holistic justice, restore relationships, affirm dignity, promote healing and allow all members of the conflicted community to share responsibility for keeping the peace.[4]

Racism and Social Conflict

Racism generates a specific, unique and multivalent brand of American social conflict. A century ago, sociologist and civil rights scholar W. E. B. DuBois, in *The Souls of Black Folks* wrote that "the problem of the twentieth century is the problem of the color-line."[5] With these words, a black man purposed to tell white America what he thought and knew from his identity as a scholar educated at Fisk University, Harvard University, and the University of Berlin.[6] In *The Souls of Black Folk*, DuBois spoke of "the meaning of being black" in his time, the meaning of legal emancipation to formerly enslaved persons and its aftermath, contending philosophies of black leadership, challenges of living in separate and unequal black-and-white worlds, and finally "to make clear the present relations of the sons of master and man."[7] His work drew upon social debt accumulated and compounded over the three centuries from the time enslaved Africans first arrived in Virginia in 1619 to the time of his writing in 1903.[8]

The barriers and burdens DuBois described called out explicit racism. Legal and sociology scholars William M. Wiecek and Judy L Hamilton explain and illustrate how explicit racism worked in "Beyond the Civil Rights Act of 1964: Confronting Structural Racism in the Workplace."

> Slavery, as a system of racial domination and subordination, was succeeded by the comprehensive racial regime that we know as segregation or Jim Crow, which lasted from the end of Reconstruction in 1877 until it began to crumble in the Second Reconstruction after 1954. Under Jim Crow, whites imposed a system of caste that assured the dominant race of superiority in all realms: social, economic, political, cultural, and legal. White supremacy was grounded in explicit racism. "Whites Only" signs policed access to public facilities, the white primary assured white political power, and segregated schools excluded people of color from all but the most minimal educational opportunity. Meanwhile, vagrancy laws, chain gangs, and convict labor created a form of crypto-slavery. Segregation ensured that opportunity was reserved for whites only and that the lot of colored races was one of inferiority, degradation, and exclusion. Explicit racism—overt, deliberated assertions of racial dominance—maintained servitude. It was this regime of oppression that the Civil Rights Act of 1964 was designed to overthrow.[9]

Explicitly racist behavior is acute and tangible. It can be identified by sight, sound, and touch.

Generally, explicit racism is defined by law. Acts of explicit racism are largely prohibited by law and, arguably, are forms of social conflict subject to management by the legal system.

Its twenty-first century successor, however is far more elusive. Structural racism is a term "sociologists use most frequently to describe the negative impact on people of color that is the product of ostensibly race-neutral policies within and among institutions."[10] In other words, it is harder to detect but no less prevalent or destructive. It is systemic, not point-specific, chronic, not acute. In a system infected by structural racism,

- There may be no intent to do harm by any individual actor in the system.
- There may be no awareness of doing harm by any individual actor in the system.
- Harm may only become apparent over time, or by using special instruments of detection.
- The harmful system persists because the system benefits entities with the power to maintain the current state of affairs.

Wiecek and Hamilton posits,

> Structural racism identifies the cause of such racial disparities in the processes, procedures, policies, historical conventions, assumptions, and beliefs regarding operational functioning that occur within, between, and among the social institutions that make up a society's infrastructure. It is the result of institutional arrangements that distribute resources unequally and inequitably.[11]

Structural racism bears similarities to infectious disease. It can spread undetected. It can cause the infected organism to malfunction, sometimes in ways leading to misdiagnosis and ineffective treatment. It can be expensive or difficult to detect, and difficult or expensive to treat. And it can be ignored, at great peril.

Explicit racism is a white man killing nine black people and telling a survivor the motivation was racial hatred. On this, there is probably widespread agreement. But are there other instances of racism in the Charleston story? If so, what are they? Are there different narratives about the meaning of this event? How was the story reported by news media? Was it reported on at all or under-reported? Was this prayed about in church communities? Included or ignored in academic discourse the following semester? Were those differences racially motivated, benign, or irrelevant? The shooting was a single act. Press coverage, church sermons, and fall syllabi, on the other hand, generate hundreds of data points available for study.

Reconciliation

Reconciliation is a difficult term to define. It is a concept in the field of restorative justice. Howard Zehr, criminologist and pioneer of the restorative justice movement, identifies three pillars of restorative justice.[12] First, restorative justice focuses on harm caused, rather than upon the offender. Next, restorative justice calls for responsibility and accountability in addressing the harm. Finally, restorative justice joins the victim, offender and the affected community together to jointly participate in remediation, or mending the breach. reconciliation require imaginative understanding of who are victims, who are offenders, and what role the Christian community has in standing with victims and offenders. Reconciliation requires truth-telling. In a racialized context, there are three concepts important to reach reconciliatory truth-telling: contested identities, challenged agency, and systemic inequity.

Contested Identities

Identity matters. In biblical texts, names are given, changed or ignored with great significance. In the workplace, job titles can matter more than job duties, and may be negotiated in addition to or in lieu of levels of compensation. Names and nomenclature can enhance or erase stature, power, dignity and respect. What identity indicators are present in the Charleston story? Are there discernable patterns? Do those patterns break upon racial lines?

Narrative also signals identity, as it constructs contexts for and gives meaning, power and voice to named elements of the story. Similarly, omissions in narrative subtract meaning, diminish power, and silence through absence and invisibility. What naming and narrative patterns emerge from the Charleston accounts? Do those patterns raise questions of race? Do those differences enhance or suppress power?

Challenged Agencies

Social psychology teaches what many understand instinctively: people want and need to be useful, purpose-filled and able to build, contribute to and maintain community. Human agency is " a combination of human capacity and potential that assists a person to exercise some control over the nature and quality of his or her own life, including aspects such a fore-thought; self-regulation of motivation; affect and action through self-influence, self-awareness, meaning and purpose in life."[13] If the concept of agency can be extended to include those who self-identify as having shared purpose and shared life beyond individual existence, then applied to the Charleston story, interesting questions arise.

- What does it mean to be part of a religious community that claims roots in centuries-old resistance to racial oppression?
- What did it mean for that community to be lead by one with both moral authority as senior pastor, but also wielded a measure of civic and political authority as an elected state legislator?
- What other autonomy questions are imbedded in this narrative, and how are they informed by race?

Systemic Inequity

Whether measuring against legal standards of due process, equal protection, and fundamental fairness, or by prophetic proclamation to do justice, love mercy, and walk humbly, there are basic indicators of equity that may clarify the narrative of challenged agency. Systemic inequity is an interplay between internal forces, such as personal bias, privilege, and internalized racism and external forces, such as interpersonal relationships, institutional racism, and structural oppression.[14] This provides explanation for different lived experiences based on race. Systemic inequity accounts for disparities in health, education, employment, and justice systems. For context, readers are encouraged to study *Unfinished Reconciliation: Justice, Racism, and Churches of Christ*, edited by theologians Gary Holloway and John York (2013) to understand ways in which systemic inequity of access, accountability, reciprocity, and respect in competing narratives of whether and how identity and agency operate in the Churches of Christ.

Process Pilgrimage

At this point, a reasonable person can be driven to a complete standstill because there seem to be far too many demons to exorcise. Many have tried and failed, returning to their base camp, muttering in defeat. If there is any encouragement at all, it might be from a still, small voice hinting something to the effect that this type of roadblock is only removed by prayer and fasting (Matt. 17:21). The conflict manager hears in this struggle a call to return to and faithfully follow the journey of faith, to continue this pilgrimage towards promise,[15] taking the long walk to freedom.[16]

Orders of worship, patterns of prayer, and liturgical devotions can calm, comfort, constrain and contain fear, anger, and pain. Conflict management processes such as coaching, mediation,[17] dialogue circles[18] and appreciative inquiry[19] are designed to elicit similar responses in narrowly defined, situation-specific contexts. By customizing processes designed to attend to the cognitive, emotional, and behavior dimensions of the specific parties in a particular dispute, a skilled conflict manager can curate a space where parties come to feel welcome, safe, and therefore willing to engage in tough work together.

No one conflict process tool is suitable for every race-and-religion conversation. Prior to engaging in the resolution process, it is necessary to engage in purification, preparation, and presence as stages towards reconciliation. Taken in order, each stage addresses critical tasks that need attending to as prerequisites for success in subsequent legs of the journey.

Purification

This stage owes more to spiritual discipline than formal conflict management theory, if not practice. Regular, consistent attention to defined daily spiritual practice may calm and center the spirit, convict one to particular action, or clarify through spiritual discernment whether, when or how to engage race-religion reconciliation. The decision to embark upon this journey should be knowing, intelligent, and voluntary. There is a saying among conflict managers that "the right answer at the wrong time is the wrong answer."[20] Irreparable harm may be done to fragile relationships already compromised by lack of trust when individuals or groups enter into this work lightly, without having counted the cost. This may include conducting a ruthless and searching inventory of our wounds, biases, anger and fear around race. The purification phase is an optimal time to have the tough and honest internal conversations that will provide foundations for integrity and trust building later.

Preparation

This is where the rubber hits the road. Whether parties in conflict come together in an attempt to negotiate differences directly, or use a neutral facilitator to help manage the process tensions between them, two tasks are essential: fact-finding and process planning. Christopher Moore, a founder of contemporary mediation practice, describes the task of collecting and analyzing background information as most critical, as conflict management interventions may fail when this step is overlook, and previous efforts ignored, duplicated, or contradicted.[21]

I offer a general strategy for tailoring information gathering relative to specific conflict conversations on race-and-religion:

- Deconstruct the conflict definition. Ask questions and seek answers about each element. For example, ask
  - Is there a struggle? Is it expressed? If so, how? What behaviors are observed?
  - What is the struggle about? Goals? Resources? Autonomy? Identity? Power?
  - What is the history between the disputing parties?
  - What is the nature of their interconnectedness?

- Deconstruct the social conflict checklist. Ask who, what, when, where, how, and why for each element.
- Deconstruct the racism definitions. Are there elements of explicit racism in this dispute? If so, repeat the who, what, when, where,

why and how analysis. Are there elements of structural racism? If so, what are they?

While the pattern of questioning may seem simple and repetitive, experience shows that the results are anything but. A methodical process of structured inquiry can reveal patterns, connections and insights that lead to clarity, understanding, and a paradoxically humbling sense that the more one learns, the less one knows. It should be understood that the task of asking questions is framed in the context of doing serious, thoughtful, and substantive work. Respect and reciprocity are useful guides. What might this mean? Collecting background information about what it is like to grow up in circumstances unlike one's own experience might mean asking one who had that experience. Or it might not if the inquiry is invasive, rude, asks another to relive embarrassment or pain, or takes advantage of vulnerability structured by the power differential between the asker and the asked. Direct questions may be insulting if asked out of laziness or arrogant disregard for the reductive nature of the ask.

How does a conflict manager collect and analyze background information at this stage? Active reading and passive listening. This process is undertaken as an immersive experience in the literature and languages of unfamiliar others. This type of information gathering includes mining histories, narratives, research reports, Twitter feeds and Facebook pages. "Reading" may also include movies, television series, and the lyrics to popular music of all genres engaged by the parties in dispute. Reading in this mode is not for entertainment or for passing judgment on content; rather, it is an objective exercise in learning what content exists.

Unlike the formal conflict resolution technique of active listening, passive listening does not reflect, reframe, or respond to the speaker. The purpose of passive listening is to hear and learn what people are saying in a resting state, or to hear what people say to each other when the listener is not centered in the conversation. It is a selfless, powered-down state of learning. A passive listener fortunate enough to be granted "read only" access to the conversation may hear scripts intentionally crafted for the listener (the public story). She may also, as time passes and trust builds, hear deeper truths and genuine narratives of self-definition (identity) and self-determination (agency).

Presence

Here, the conflict manager turns to the Bible for instruction in the power of presence as a precursor to restoration and reconciliation. She reads the travels of Naomi and Ruth, the mobile classroom of Jesus, and the twelve apostles, and the capstone exercises of her seventy graduate students sent out in pairs to test theory in the field as examples of three important principles. First, learning journeys take time. Second, travelers learn from each other, and learn to trust each other. Third, learning journeys include breaks for hospitality, where gifts of generosity and grace can manifest. Journeys to places of special significance mark history, and recalls narratives of identity, agency and justice.

On Wednesday, June 17, 2015, important work was interrupted but not derailed. White and black Christians, and anyone who identifies as a member of the beloved community,[22] may wish to consider what it means to be committed to journey together through seasons of wondering together, walking together, working together, and waiting together until reconciliation reconsiders us.

In the immediate context of conversations between black and white Christians, there are a few resources that deserve special emphasis. Below are additional online resources to enhance your study of the reconciliation process.

Notes

[1] Marke Berman, "I Forgive You. Relatives of Charleston Church Shooting Victims Address Dylann Roof," accessed March 21, 2016, https://www.washingtonpost.com/news/post-nation/wp/2015/06/19/i-forgive-you-relatives-of-charleston-church-victims-address-dylann-roof/.

[2] Elizabeth Bruening, "Should We Forgive Dylann Roof? The Roots and Purpose of Christian Forgiveness," accessed March 21, 2016, https://newrepublic.com/article/122109/should-we-forgive-dylann-roof/.

[3] William W.Wilmot and Joyce L. Hocker, *Interpersonal Conflict*. 5th ed. (Boston: McGraw-Hill, 1998).

[4] Adapted from Louis Kriesberg and Bruce W. Dayton, *Constructive Conflicts: From Escalation to Resolution*, fourth ed. (Lanham, MD: Rowman and Littlefield Publishers, Inc., 2012), 3–6.

[5] William Edward Burghardt. DuBois, *The Souls of Black Folk: Essays and Sketches*, (McClurg, 1909), 13.

[6] Phillip Luke Sinitiere, "Leadership for Democracy and Peace: W. E. B. Du Bois's Legacy as a Pan-African Intellectual." in *Leadership in Colonial Africa*, Palgrave Studies in African Leadership, ed. Baba G. Jallow (Palgrave Macmillan US, 2014). 153–81.

[7] DuBois, *The Souls of Black Folk*, viii.

[8] See, Historic Jamestown National Park Service website (http://www.nps.gov/jame/learn/historyculture/african-americans-at-jamestown.htm/. accessed 2/22/2016.

[9] William M. Wiecek, and Judy L Hamilton. "Beyond the Civil Rights Act of 1964: Confronting Structural Racism in the Workplace." *LA Law. Review* 74 (2013): 1099.

[10] Ibid, 1103.

[11] Ibid, 1106.

[12] Howard Zehr, *The Little Book of Restorative Justice*, Revised and Updated (Skyhorse Publishing, Inc., 2015).

[13] Charles P. Chen "Strengthening Career Human Agency," *Journal of Counseling and Development* 84,2 (2006): 131.

[14] Sonia Ospina and Erica Gabrielle Foldy. "Toward a Framework of Social Change Leadership," *SSRN Scholarly Paper* (September 1, 2005), accessed 2/25/2016, http://papers.ssrn.com/abstract=1532332/.

[15] Some may read this hearing Albert A. Goodson's song, "We've Come This Far by Faith," (Manna Music, Inc., 1963).

[16] Others may read this and think of the Underground Railroad, or hear James Weldon Johnson's anthem, "Lift Every Voice and Sing," (1921).

[17] On the definitive and exhaustive work of Christopher Moore in his *The Mediation Process: Practical Strategies for Resolving Conflict* (Wiley, 2014).

[18] The Public Conversations Project offers excellent resources for fostering dialogue "where conversations are driven by differences in identity, beliefs, and values." See http://publicconversations.org/.

[19] Appreciative inquiry is a discipline of positive change Resources and reading lists are available at https://appreciativeinquiry.case.edu/.

[20] Though available for fair use, I choose to credit the saying to my former mediation professor, Tracy Allen.

[21]Christopher W Moore, *The Mediation Process:* (Wiley, 2014). 111.

[22]See the summary of the Beloved Community in "Unveiling Radical Love" by Stanley Tolbert in this volume.

[23]This information may be followed on Twitter (#charlestonsyllabus), or at the African American Intellectual History Society website: http://www.aaihs.org/resources /charlestonsyllabus/.

Additional Online Resources

Charleston Syllabus (#charlestonsyllabus)
Conceived by Brandeis University professor Chad Williams, the hashtag launched two days after the shooting and served as both a beacon to attract contributions from scholars, and an anchor in collecting and curating sources for scholarship on myriad topics related to the shooting, its historical context, and the communities and cultures it attacked.[23] The bibliography covers the following topics:

- General historic overviews,
- Readings on South Carolina
- Charleston
- Slavery
- Slavery in the US South
- Slavery in the US North
- Slavery in the Atlantic World
- Readings on the Civil War & Reconstruction
- Readings on the Confederate Flag
- Readings on Post-Construction and Jim Crow
- Readings on Racial Violence
- Readings on White Racial Identity
- Readings on White Supremacy in the US and Abroad
- Readings on Race and Religion
- Readings on African American Women's Religious History
- Readings on the Civil Rights-Black Power Era
- African American Literature
- Selected Primary Sources
- Films
- Music
- Websites
- Course Handouts and Other Teaching Sources
- Young Readers

Other Websites

Disciples of Christ—maintains a full website (www.reconciliationministry .org) devoted to ministry in reconciliation, restorative justice, a resource guide to Ferguson, Mo, and structural racism as manifest in the "School-to-Prison pipeline".

Southern Baptist Resolution on Race—posts on its general website (www .sbc.net) the Resolution on Racial Reconciliation on the 150th Anniversary of the Southern Baptist Convention (1995).

United Methodist Church—maintains a full website (www.gcorr.org) for the General Commission on Religion and Race. Includes links to 9Tips for Fostering Vital Conversations and Appreciative Inquiry.

Episcopal Church—maintains resources on two websites (www .episcopalarchives.org and Episcopalchurch.org). The historical archive contains links to documents on the churches' history of internal racism, and a timeline ending with a 1994 Pastoral Letter condemning the 'sin of racism." This website includes a page for Racial Reconciliation, with blogs titled Racial Reconciliation Blog, and Blog: Away Forward: Reflections, Resources & Stories Concerning Ferguson, Racial Justice & Reconciliation.

Contributors

David Fleer is professor of Bible and Communication and Special Assistant to the President at Lipscomb University. He is the Director of the Christian Scholars Conference and author/editor of several books including *Preaching John's Gospel: The World It Imagines*, *Reclaiming the Imagination: The Exodus as Paradigmatic Narrative for Preaching*, and *Preaching Autobiography: Connecting the World of Preacher and the World of the Text*.

Doug Foster is professor of Church History and Director of the Center for Restoration Studies at Abilene Christian University. He is the author or editor of over eleven books including *The Story of the Churches of Christ*, *Renewing the World: A Concise Global History of the Stone-Campbell Movement*, and *The Encyclopedia of the Stone-Campbell Movement*.

Phyllis Hildreth is the Academic Director of the Institute for Conflict Management, as well as an adjunct professor for the Institute for Law, Justice and Society at Lipscomb University. Hildreth also serves in Nashville as a Court Appointed Special Advocate (CASA), as a member of The Women's Fund, and the Girl Scouts of Middle Tennessee.

Richard Hughes is Scholar in Residence in the College of Bible and Ministry at Lipscomb University. He is the author or editor of seventeen books including *Reviving the Ancient Faith: The Story of Churches of Christ in America*, *Myths America Lives By*, *Christian America and the Kingdom of God*, and *The Vocation of a Christian Scholar: How Christian Faith Can Sustain the Life of the Mind*.

Brad McKinnon is assistant professor of history and ministry and serves as Director of Christian Service, Dean of Students, and Director of Chapel Programs at Heritage Christian University.

Don McLaughlin is the pulpit minister of North Atlanta Church of Christ, Atlanta, Georgia. He conducts seminars and workshops on spiritual growth, communication, leadership, and personal effectiveness in the US and around the world, and is the author of *Heaven in the Real World*.

Yukikazu Obata is adjunct lecturer at Ibaraki Christian University. Born and raised in Tokyo, Japan, Obata serves as a minister at the Mito Church of Christ and is a doctoral candidate completing his PhD in Intercultural Studies at Fuller Theological Seminary, writing a dissertation on pre-WWII Church of Christ missions in the context of imperial Japan.

Lawrence Rodgers is an MDiv student at Howard University's School of Divinity, and serves as a ministering evangelist at the Westside Church of Christ in Baltimore, Maryland.

Jerry Taylor is associate professor of Bible at Abilene Christian University, Abilene, Texas. He is the author of *Courageous Compassion: A Prophetic Homiletic in Service to the Church*.

Stanley Tyrone Talbert is a doctoral student at Union Theological Seminary. He also serves as an assistant minister at the Kings Church of Christ in Brooklyn, New York. A recent participant of Union's Millennial Leaders Project, Tolbert is a contributor to the *Huffington Post*. Tolbert recently completed his master's thesis, from Union, entitled, "Beyond Nonviolence: A Theological Account of Systemic Violence in the Age of the New Jim Crow."

John Mark Tucker is retired Dean of Library and Information Resources at Abilene Christian University and Professor Emeritus of Library Science at Purdue University.

William Lofton Turner is Distinguished Professor in the College of Leadership and Public Service and is Counselor to the President at Lipscomb University. A Robert Woods Johnson Health Policy Fellow, Turner helped to shape important health policy for then–Senator Barack Obama.

CPSIA information can be obtained
at www.ICGtesting.com
Printed in the USA
FSOW03n0058060716
22299FS